S0-AJX-404

ESTATE PLANNING IS DEAD!

Asset Protection Planning is Alive and Well
(A Consumer's Guide to Modern Estate Planning)

Reed K. Scott, MBA, JD, LL.M. (Tax)

Copyright © 2013 Reed K. Scott. All rights reserved. No portion of this book may be reproduced mechanically, electronically, or by any other means, including photocopying, without written permission of the publisher. It is illegal to copy this book, post it to a website, or distribute it by any other means without permission from the publisher.

Reed K. Scott
E-mail: reed@yesllp.com
Website: www.yesllp.com

Limits of Liability and Disclaimer of Warranty
The author and publisher shall not be liable for your misuse of this material. This book is strictly for informational and educational purposes.

Warning – Disclaimer
The purpose of this book is to educate and entertain. The author and/or publisher do not guarantee that anyone following these techniques, suggestions, tips, ideas, or strategies will have a successful outcome. The author and/or publisher shall have neither liability nor responsibility to anyone with respect to any loss or damage caused, or alleged to be caused, directly or indirectly by the information contained in this book.

Second Edition
Previously published as *The Cinderella Estate Plan: How to Protect Your Children's Inheritance (A Consumer's Guide to Modern Estate Planning)*

For access to more insights on wealth planning, tax savings strategies, business planning, asset protection and more, visit www.yesllp.com and register for a free weekly e-mail newsletter and blog.

"Reed has a rare talent for turning a complicated subject into an exciting and fun-to-read topic. I recommend this book to all my clients."
Kelly Crane, CFP, CFATM, CLU
Napa Valley Wealth Management

"Reed has unlocked the secrets of protecting your family's wealth and put them into simple-to-understand steps. Whether you care about the legacy you leave behind for your family or if you just want to want to make sure your assets are protected during your lifetime, this book is a must read."
Julie Posey, Financial Advisor

"These are subjects not normally covered in the dry pages of the average estate planning manual. This is a must read for everyone who wants to cover all of the bases- even the ones you most often do not think about."
David J. Stull, CLU, ChFC – The Stull Financial Group

"This book is *THE* book that every family must have. I tell my clients to read this book and save your family a ton of grief and a ton of money."
William Burke, CLU, CFP
Past President San Francisco Estate Planning Council

My heartfelt appreciation to my clients, who have trusted me to help them protect their assets, build their businesses, their wealth, and their dreams, and to my daughter, Lauren, for giving me the inspiration to always pursue my dreams.

About the Author

Reed Scott is an attorney, who in addition to his law degree, has an MBA in finance and a master's in tax law. He has been a financial analyst for Ford Motor Corporation, and corporate counsel and president for a technology consulting company based in San Francisco. He is managing partner at a respected law firm in Northern California. His firm focuses on asset protection, tax and wealth planning for individuals and businesses.

Reed was originally drawn to asset protection planning because he saw his clients spend years and often decades trying to accumulate wealth and avoid taxes only to lose everything due to unexpected circumstances and things that seemed outside of their control. After much research and experience he began to develop techniques for protecting families and businesses from the unexpected. He began showing people that what seems outside of our control doesn't have to be. After working with thousands of families it became clear that the entire estate planning industry was not serving modern families. The things that eat up modern family wealth have nothing to do with what most consumers expect. Reed wrote this book to save families from the devastating costs of poor traditional and outdated estate planning. Estate planning, in his opinion, is still about 100 years behind the times.

Reed's law firm, Youngman Ericsson Scott, LLP, has over 9,000 clients in California, and provides a full range of services to business owners and families.

He is a sought-after speaker who gives dynamic seminars on wealth planning and asset protection, and has educated thousands of business owners, professionals and consumers on estate planning, tax, and asset protection techniques.

Reed has developed a system for protecting family wealth and helping to prevent the types of things that can lead to wealth erosion after the death of a first spouse or upon transfer to children.

He also developed a system for building and protecting retirement accounts that he has implemented for hundreds of his clients, and written a separate book on that method (available at www.yesllp.com).

Reed also wrote a nursing home guide for California that explains how to qualify for financial assistance for nursing home costs without going broke, and provides a guide to and information on available nursing homes in California (also available at www.yesllp.com).

FREE THIRTY MINUTE CONSULTATION!

If you've read one of my books and you'd like to set up an asset protection plan for your family, and you're a California resident, then email me at reed@yesllp.com and to schedule a complimentary Skype consultation. See the end of this book for how to take advantage of this offer.

FREE E-BOOK!
"RETIREMENT ACCOUNT RICHES"

Learn how to turn a $350,000 retirement account into a multimillion dollar family dynasty!

"Retirement Account Riches" is a book that shows you how to make sure your retirement accounts can minimize taxes and maximize value!

Most Americans don't realize the power the tax code gives them to create wealth. Quit complaining about taxes and use them to your advantage! This book details just how to do that.

Learn how to avoid the critical mistakes people make in their retirement accounts. Make sure you download your **FREE** copy today from **www.yesllp.com.**

Contents

Introduction
Estate Planning is Dead!

W
hat do I mean when I say estate planning is dead? Do I mean that you shouldn't do estate planning? In a way, yes. You should NOT do traditional estate planning, which the large majority of Americans are still doing when they meet with their traditional estate planning attorneys and financial advisors. They sit and talk about taxes and transferring assets at death, but they ignore the things that are destroying families in a modern society. They do nothing to protect a family's assets from the modern enemies of family wealth.

The legal and financial services industries are very traditional and slow to change. While medical technology and science have advanced exponentially in the last fifty years, many planners are still using planning techniques that are, in my opinion, woefully obsolete.

Most estate plans I see (even recent ones) don't do anything to protect you and your family. The purpose of this book is to alert you to what I believe are the **three biggest planning mistakes** that I see in most estate plans today.

Why do people even do estate planning? After all, we won't be here, so what does it matter? Most people think they are doing something for others when they think about estate planning, and many of us may not be as motivated to help others in the future as we are to take care of ourselves in the present.

The problem is that when most people think of their own death, they envision passing peacefully in their sleep. No muss, no fuss, and certainly no preceding three, five, or even 10 years of dementia or Alzheimer's disease where a spouse or children have had to care for them.

Thanks to modern medicine and science, however, our ever-increasing life expectancies are getting to the point that the only thing that will keep most of us from getting a debilitating old age disease will be if we die first. With modern technology, it is more and more likely you won't die first.

This book wasn't written to scare you. In fact, I hope that you take care of yourself, eat right, exercise, and live the best possible life as long as you can.

In our DNA there are diseases lurking and waiting to come out. Whether it's Parkinson's, heart problems, dementia, Alzheimer's, or debilitating diseases like Multiple Sclerosis, the longer we live, the more likely our DNA will betray us. The fact that your family has no history of these illnesses may simply mean they just didn't live long enough.

Is it really bad news that we're living longer? Of course not! It's great that we can live longer and experience all life has to offer. In fact, scientists predict that based on population trends 20-year-olds today are three times more likely to reach 100 than their grandparents, and twice as likely as their parents.

This doesn't even take into account the fact that today people who are in severe accidents that would have meant certain death 50 years ago may instead live in a long period of incapacity thanks to modern technology.

For example, it wasn't that long ago that if you had an accident and couldn't eat or drink by swallowing, you were going to die. It was just that simple. Then, in the 1970s, medicine developed feeding tubes, which has led to some of the most horrific legal battles of our times (for example, the famous Terri Schiavo case in Florida).

Unfortunately, the legal profession hasn't been quite as innovative as medicine and science.

Introduction

While scientists were busy solving the mysteries of the DNA helix, lawyers were doing what they always do: using the same documents they had been using for the last 100 years. After all, the legal profession is not about innovation; it's about safety, tradition, and respect for "the law."

Well, over the last 100 years while the average life expectancy has gone from less than 50 to almost 80, most Americans have continued planning their estates around traditional death documents. They've been oblivious to the three biggest things that actually destroy their wealth and their families' peace of mind:

1. Devastating healthcare expenses,
2. Remarriages after the death of the first spouse, and
3. Your children's own divorce or death before their spouse.

So the good news is we're living longer. The bad news is we aren't prepared for it. Most estate planning documents I see today, whether they were drafted recently or 20 years ago, seem to be more focused on death and taxes than the big three I mentioned above.

The consequences of poor planning mean that you or your spouse may not have enough money to provide for your long-term care in the event of a devastating illness. Even if you don't have a devastating illness and you die suddenly and leave everything to your spouse, he or she is now much more likely to live a long time after your death. Due to longer life spans, more widows and widowers are remarrying after the death of a spouse.

How does the remarriage of your spouse affect the children of the first marriage? What if your spouse dies before his or her new spouse? Did your spouse take care to keep the assets separate? Did he or she get a pre-nuptial agreement? Did he or she end up living in a community property state? Does he or she have a separate trust for his or her assets to make sure everything you worked for all your life doesn't go to a stranger and the stranger's children? This is where your children can end up like Cinderella, with everything going to their step brothers and sisters.

And what if your spouse does protect the assets you worked so hard to accumulate over your lifetime and they do make it to your children? What happens if your son or daughter gets divorced? What happens if none of that happens but your son or daughter happens to die before his or her spouse? Will the inheritance that you intended for your grandchildren go to the step-children of your daughter or son-in-law?

Did you notice I didn't ask about taxes or probates? That's because taxes and death probates are not what destroy estates anymore. It's now the big three described above.

All of the them are a direct result of longer life spans. You or your spouse need to protect your assets from devastating healthcare costs, yet there are no provisions in your plan to allow for asset protection. You and your spouse may live longer, but there are no provisions in your plan to accommodate a remarriage. Your children have a longer life expectancy than you, but your plan fails to protect them in the event of a divorce and remarriage.

To add fuel to the fire, while your estate planning issues have become more complex, we live in a time where everyone has instant access to information. With the internet and social media there is no better time for the unscrupulous to take advantage of the unwary. If I were an uncaring attorney, I could just plug your name into the same old boilerplate documents that have been around for years and send you on your way. You wouldn't know you didn't have a plan that works until your family has to deal with the mess.

In my opinion, this is why I see so many bad plans when clients come in to update the estate plan they had prepared elsewhere. After all, it's an easy way to make money off someone who can't complain in the future because they are either incapacitated or dead.

Even car dealers have to deal with lemon laws, but people can sell you estate planning documents over the internet with impunity. Attorneys with little to no experience in this area, who don't even handle trust administrations, are willing to plug your name into a template file for some extra revenue. When your family calls them for assistance upon your incapacity or death the attorney can say: "You need to go somewhere else. I don't deal with trust administrations. I just create the trusts; I don't implement them." And of course, there is no one available to help your family with trust administration at the website where Mom and Dad bought the trust for $99. (Now you know why it was such a good deal.) There is no one looking out for your family except you.

That is why I wrote this book. It's important that you, as a consumer, are educated and understand what to look for when planning your estate. And what you need to know isn't primarily about taxes and legal statutes. It's about thinking about the real, everyday things that happen in our families and how to make sure our families are protected from the bad so they can enjoy the good. You hire an attorney for their expertise and experience, not for their ability to copy and paste. By having me share my expertise and experience with you, you will be better able to judge someone you are considering to help you plan your family's ultimate instruction manual: your estate plan. If your advisors aren't talking to you about these issues, why not?

My hope is that this book will lead you to think about your own family and help you put a plan in place that actually works. Too many times I have seen what poor planning can do to families or single people with no one to care for them. If this book can spare one family or one person that heartache, it will have achieved its purpose.

I always tell my clients that good estate planning (or what I prefer to call asset protection planning) is like time travel: You have to go into the future and visualize what you want to happen for your spouse, your children, and your grandchildren, and then we have to build your time machine—your family asset protection plan. There are the traditional time machines that have been taking families into the past and there are modern time machines that can take families into the future. Make sure your time machine is built for the future you want your family to experience.

Definitions

This book is not designed to be a book of technical jargon on estate planning. It is meant to be conversational and full of examples. However, just to make sure everyone is on the same page I am going to briefly define a few basic terms.

1. **Revocable Trust:** A legal document typically used for estate planning purposes. The term *revocable* means it can be changed during your lifetime. It can be used to avoid state involvement in your affairs by opting out of the state probate system. Unlike a will, a trust holds legal title to your assets and allows them to be privately transferred to your heirs at your death. Unlike a will, the revocable trust can also be used to have someone you trust manage your financial affairs during incapacity.

2. **Living Trust:** An often-used synonym for a revocable trust. It is just a common name for a revocable trust.

3. **Irrevocable Trust:** A trust that cannot be easily changed. Often used for asset protection and tax planning.

4. **Will:** A document designed to be taken to court to tell the court what who you want to have your assets upon your death.

5. **Pour-Over Will:** An abbreviated will that is used in conjunction with a revocable trust and is designed to only be used if you forget to title an asset correctly in the name of your revocable trust.

6. **Durable or Financial Powers of Attorney:** A legal document designed to give someone power to control your assets if you

are incapacitated. Not as reliable as a trust because a financial power of attorney does not hold legal title to your assets.

7. **Healthcare Directive or Healthcare Power of Attorney:** A legal document appointing someone as agent to make healthcare decisions for you if you are not able to communicate with medical professionals at the time of need.

8. **HIPAA (Health Insurance Portability and Accountability Act):** A federal law designed to protect the unauthorized release of your personal medical information. You must give your agents and your trustees in your estate plan written authority to talk to your doctors on your behalf.

9. **Medicare:** The federal government health insurance program for Americans age 65 and older.

10. **Medicaid:** The combined state and federal program designed to provide healthcare services to people based upon their inability to pay for their own care. (This program is called Medicaid in 49 states and called Medi-Cal in California.)

Section I
Times Have Changed

"The future belongs to those who prepare for it today."
~ Malcolm X

Chapter 1
How Much for a Trust?

How much do you charge for a trust? This is the extent of the research that most people do when they are looking for an estate plan. This is the question my assistant gets most often from people calling when they are shopping for attorneys to do their estate planning. It is often the only question. My answer: It depends, but we give a range that will vary based on the circumstances. Most of the time my range is too high for people shopping based on price alone. However, people who know me and are referred by friends, family members, CPAs, financial advisors, and other attorneys and professionals don't even ask the price. They know that what I do has true value and what I charge is a bargain for what they get: *peace of mind*.

Congratulations! If you're reading this book it means you are part of a small percentage of Americans who care enough about your family to make sure you have the very best possible estate plan in place for your loved ones. You're not just looking for cheap, you're looking for value—a plan that accomplishes your objectives and works the way you intended. You know you get what you pay for, and if something sounds too good to be true, it usually is.

Why do I say a small percentage? Because statistics tell us that only about 30 percent of Americans have done any type of estate planning. Of that 30 percent, I'd be willing to make a substantial wager that at least half of those plans aren't worth the paper they're written on (and I think I'm being generous).

You may be thinking to yourself at this point that maybe the statistic is because 70 percent of Americans don't have enough wealth to necessitate an estate plan. That may be part of the reason, but I can assure you from my own experience it is not the whole story. Half of the clients that come to me every month have no planning documents in place. The other half of the clients have some kind of a plan in place, but no one has reviewed it in years and it is often woefully out of date. All of these people have known they needed a plan for years but have gone without one for a variety of reasons.

It's natural to not want to face the unpleasant reality of our own mortality, so we put it off by denying it for as long as possible and delaying planning. Even though it doesn't make intellectual sense, what better way to deny the inevitable than to not do the essential planning that we know must be done? After all, if we don't talk about death, maybe it won't notice us and move on to someone else.

Don't Just Check the Box

Often when people do get around to planning, they want to get it over with as cheaply and as quickly as possible. They want to feel good about themselves and check off the box so they can say they've done the right thing. They might get a recommendation for an attorney from a neighbor, co-worker, or their financial advisor, and that is the extent of their investigation.

A wise man once said: "The strangest thing of all is that everyone knows death is inevitable, but no one thinks it is going to happen to them!"

Another reason people don't do proper estate planning is that they just simply don't realize what estate planning is and how essential it is that every person have a well-thought-out and fully documented plan. As an attorney that provides estate planning AND administration, I often tend to take for granted that everyone knows what estate planning is and understands the process. I have come to find out the hard way, however, that this is not the case.

If you're thinking there is some magic dollar amount your estate must be before you start estate planning, forget it. There is no magic number. If you have any assets at all, you need an estate plan to control those assets. Even if you don't have any assets or wealth you still need a plan to give legal authority to someone who can oversee your physical person if you are too sick to speak for yourself (a healthcare directive).

Estate planning can mean a lot of different things depending on the circumstances. Financial advisors often use the term to talk about building and managing your wealth. From a legal perspective, however, estate planning means much more than just managing your assets. And of course, financial advisors cannot legally draft legal documents, so when they refer to estate planning it has a different meaning.

A legal estate plan means that you have actual legal documents executed, in place, and up-to-date that tell us exactly who is in charge of your physical assets and your physical person in the event of your incapacity or your death. A good plan will also make sure that all the things you own (real estate, bank accounts, retirement plans, life insurance, etc.) are titled in a manner that is consistent with your plan. (I can't tell you how many people come to me with existing trusts where their assets are titled in a manner that is completely inconsistent with their wishes.) In my opinion, **a modern estate plan goes a step beyond the basic and actually does things to protect your assets.**

When most people think about estate planning they think about what happens when they die, but they completely forget that, as we age, the higher the probability that we will have a period of incapacity before we die.

My doctor told me, "Reed, the only thing that will keep each and every one of us from getting Alzheimer's, dementia, Parkinson's, or some other old age disease is that some of us will die before the symptoms have a chance to come out." When I asked my doctor what he meant by that statement, he explained that all of us have imperfect

DNA, and that the longer we live, the higher the probability that one or more of the old age diseases will begin to "come out" of our DNA and manifest in our bodies.

The good news is that the latest Census Bureau data shows that more and more Americans are living to 100. In fact, the centenarian population has grown 65.8 percent over the past three decades, from 32,194 people who were age 100 or older in 1980 to 53,364 centenarians in 2010. The total population has only increased 36.3 percent over the same time period. The rate of growth of people living to 100 in the United States is almost double the general population growth!

That's the good news, but the bad news is what my doctor told me: as more and more of us are living longer, the greater the probability that we will contract an "old age" disease before we die.

The Modern Dilemma

Here is a scenario that is happening more and more across America. One of my clients came to me whose father had been diagnosed with Alzheimer's. Her father's doctor had told the daughter that her father could no longer manage his affairs and that she needed to take over his day-to-day finances. (Her mother had died several years earlier.) Upon reviewing her dad's estate planning documents, which had been drafted by another attorney a few years before, we found that the daughter would need two written statements from physicians stating what the doctor had already said: that her father was unable to manage his affairs. (This is often the case in trusts and powers of attorneys - a successor trustee or power of attorney agent can't take charge without proof of incapacity.)

Unfortunately, her dad's doctor told her that he was uncomfortable providing such a statement for liability reasons. Imagine my client's surprise and anger when the very same doctor that told her that her father was unable to manage his own affairs refused to give her a written statement to that effect!

By the way, if you think this is a rare occurrence, think again.

14

It is happening more and more across America as legal estate planning documents that were primarily intended to plan for death are running head-on into the reality of modern medicine.

But wait, there's more. Not only did the daughter need to take control of her father's assets and manage his finances, but she also needed to figure out how to pay for his stay in the Alzeimer's unit of a nursing home, where the costs were over $10,000/month.

Her father had around $200,000 in a savings account and still had his house, but she knew that his money wouldn't last long, given his monthly nursing home bill. She wanted me to help her qualify for some type of government assistance to help pay for his care. She was shocked to find out Medicare would not pay for her dad's nursing home bills. She didn't understand why since Medicare had been paying for his medical bills up to that point.

Her dad's doctor had told her that, despite her dad's Alzheimer's, he was physically very healthy and in all probability he would live for many years with the disease. My client was worried that she would have to start paying the bills when her dad's money ran out, and she had two children to still put through college.

Sadly, I had to tell my client that her dad's estate planning documents (his trust and power of attorneys) did not have any provisions for applying for government assistance. (The government program that can help pay for nursing home costs is called Medicaid, or Medi-Cal in California). Medicare does not pay for long-term stays in a nursing home. I will discuss this more in Chapter 4.

Medicaid Triggers

Her dad's documents needed to have "Medicaid Triggers" that would allow her to reposition her dad's assets so he could qualify for assistance, and unfortunately, they did not have these important provisions. This is a form of asset protection planning that most traditional estate planning trusts and powers of attorneys don't have.

So what options did my client have? If she couldn't find two physicians who would provide her with written statements of incapacity, she would need to go to court to seek a conservatorship to take over her dad's financial affairs. A conservatorship (sometimes called a guardianship, depending on the jurisdiction) is a tedious legal process where the person seeking the conservatorship has to demonstrate to a judge that the person cannot manage his or her affairs and that it is in the best interest of the incapacitated individual to have someone else look after his or her financial affairs. The person seeking the conservatorship has to provide complete and detailed financial information, medical testimony proving incapacity, and a plan for how the assets will be used on behalf of the incapacitated person. If a conservatorship is granted, the conservator then has to return to court on at least an annual basis and explain to the court what he or she has done and why. There are two types of conservatorships or guardianships, one for finances and one for control of the physical person.

How frustrating for a spouse or a child to have to go through this expensive, tedious, and humiliating legal process when all he or she is trying to do is the right thing. But, of course, the court doesn't know who you are or what you are trying to do, so it has to protect the incapacitated individual.

Fortunately for my client, after many weeks of frustration, she was finally able to convince the original physician to give her a written statement. She was also able to find someone else to provide the second statement necessitated by her father's estate planning documents. Of course, my client had a job, and minor children she was also trying to take care of while all this was going on.

Even though my client finally found a way to be able to manage her dad's finances, she still did not have the authority to do Medicaid planning. That was another expensive court process, as she needed to get the court's permission to take certain actions to qualify her father for government assistant to pay for his care. Courts may or may not grant permission, based upon the circumstances. This whole court process could have been avoided if the documents had included provisions allowing the successor trustee and power of attorney agent to take the actions upon incapacity.

The amazing thing was that my client's father had thought he had his affairs in order. In fact, he had even proudly told his daughter, "I made sure you would be in charge if anything happens to me. I made you my successor trustee so you can take over if anything happens to me." Even more unfortunate is that my client's father didn't do an estate plan over the internet; he went to a fully licensed attorney recommended by someone at his church. This "plan" ended up costing him and his daughter tens of thousands of dollars more than necessary, not to mention the additional stress and frustration.

What was truly unfortunate, however, was that my client's dad almost came to me to create his plan a few years before, but my client couldn't convince him to pay the extra money. He saved a thousand dollars doing his plan with that other attorney. My client's words to me after the fact were: "I should have paid for his plan for him." It made me think of all the times people have called into my office and asked, "How much for a trust?"

Now if you've read the above and think, "But none of that applies to me. My parents are deceased, I'm healthy, I don't have children, and I don't have many assets to worry about a good estate plan. Any plan is good for me," then think about this:

Because of the changes in our society and the advances in medical science, we are not only seeing nightmare scenarios like the one just discussed, but it can happen to anyone. Terri Schiavo was alive but on life support for over 12 years. If you think estate planning is just for older people with a lot of money, remember Terri Schiavo was 26 when she was placed on life support.

Nightmare on Elm Street

Let me give you another example to demonstrate why a good estate plan is necessary for everyone at any age. I call this the real Nightmare on Elm Street. I call it real because it is much more likely to happen than an attack by Freddie Krueger.

A married couple with two minor children take a well-deserved break from the children and go out for dinner and a movie. The children are at home, supervised by a babysitter who lives down the street, and the babysitter's mom is available if there is a serious problem.

This is a very responsible couple who has done their estate planning with a well-known attorney in town. He is good friends with the couple; the wives went to school together, and their children go to the same school. You just can't ask for a better background for your attorney, can you?

Unfortunately, this attorney didn't have a lot of experience with trust administration, incapacity planning, or planning for minor children. Even more unfortunate, on their way home from the movies that night, the couple had a horrible car accident. A drunk driver swerved into their lane. The crash killed the husband almost on impact, but the wife survived in a coma. She was in a coma for several weeks. The good news is that she eventually recovered fully; the bad news is what her children had to go through in the interim.

When the attorney prepared their estate plan the couple commented how thorough and conscientious he was. He had made them select guardians for their minor children, and he had helped them select trustees to manage the children's trust until they reached age 21 and could have the money outright. What he neglected to do, however, was counsel them about what would happen if they were incapacitated and unable to take care of the children. He created the traditional "death documents" that are still prevalent and in use today.

Guardians were appointed upon the death of both parents but nothing was stated upon who would be guardians during the incapacity of a surviving parent. There were no temporary guardianship documents created to supplement the "death documents."

When the couple didn't arrive home at 10:00 PM as they had stated they would, it was not a big deal. The babysitter stayed a little longer. When they didn't get home by 11:00 PM, however, the babysitter became concerned and called her mom. Her mom came over and took over, because the babysitter had to go to school the next day. Around midnight the neighbor got a visit from the police and a

Child Protective Services (CPS) custody officer. The neighbor said that she was more than willing to take and watch the children until a family member could get there, but the police had no authority to make such a decision. In cases where no one locally has been given temporary guardianship with written authority, the minor children must be taken into protective custody.

The next day, Grandma arrived from Florida. She got in late, so she couldn't see the children until the following day. Remember: This couple had thought they had been responsible. They told Grandma she had been appointed guardian, and that their estate planning documents were in the safe in their closet. They told Grandma where the key was to the safe, and she got the documents and headed off to Child Protective Services as soon as humanly possible. CPS told her that the document she had appointing her as guardian was a will and that a will is a death document that need to be admitted to probate. Probate is a court proceeding where, in this case, the court approves the couple's selection of a guardian.

You may be asking at this point, "What about the trust? I thought a trust avoided probate." While it is true a trust can avoid probate on the control of financial assets, a trust cannot appoint guardians for minor children. The appointment of guardians for minor children is made in a will and then, upon the death of the parents, the will must be submitted to the court so the court can approve the appointed guardians. Anytime minor children are involved the state takes a protective stance. Even though a parent can select and appoint their own guardians in their legal documents, they still must be approved by the court. If there are no issues with the guardians they will be approved, but the process must still happen.

In this case, however, what happens to the children while their mom is in a coma? Well, if her attorney had created temporary guardianship papers that would appoint Grandma as guardian during incapacity, then Grandma could have gotten immediate control of the children. Even better, if the attorney had counseled the couple on what happens in the above situation, they could have appointed a local temporary guardian that could have taken the children immediately so they wouldn't have to go into protective custody in the first place. The couple could have given the babysitter's mom a convenient emergency contact card with the temporary guardian's name and number so the guardian could have been the first person to arrive on the scene.

Grandma could have been named as a temporary guardian as well so the local temporary guardian can relinquish her authority when Grandma arrives. This keeps the children out of state custody for even one night. The temporary guardianship would allow Grandma to take legal control of the children until a permanent appointment could be approved through the courts if Mom did not awake from the coma.

I know, I know. You are reading this and thinking, "Reed, I have no minor children. It's just me and my husband (or you're single). My parents are deceased, and we own everything in joint tenancy or community property. Why do I need any estate planning? When my spouse dies everything goes to me automatically and vice versa. The heck with my adult children. They can go through probate when we both die and get what's left (or you don't have any children)."

That sounds reasonable, except you forgot about the example above where a child can do Medicaid planning to protect your assets and keep you from going broke if you have a severe illness. And what about just between spouses? What if one spouse has a severe illness and needs long-term care? Do you have long-term care insurance? Is it enough? Often these policies are limited in scope.

Let's defer the Medicaid planning issue between spouses until later. The real question is: if a married couple owns everything jointly, do they need estate planning? I hear the question a lot, and my answer is this: what happens if one of you has a stroke, accident, or other illness that causes you to be incapacitated? Does your deed say community property with rights upon incapacity? No, it doesn't. It says joint tenancy or community property with "rights of survivorship." This means that if one spouse is unable to sign, certain assets (like real estate) will effectively be in limbo. The well spouse will not be able to sell, refinance, or get an equity line on real estate. If the well spouse needs to do something with the real estate to help pay for the care of the incapacitated spouse, the other spouse will have to get a conservatorship to gain the court's approval for that transaction.

Maybe the well spouse can get money out of the ill spouse's IRA or 401k plan to cover medical bills? Unfortunately, when you call the company that holds the account, you find out you are only a beneficiary. You get the money when the ill spouse dies, but not while he or she is incapacitated. This leaves us with the unpleasant necessity of having to go to court in a conservatorship hearing to ask for permission to use our own money.

This doesn't sound like an appealing solution to me, and to most people I know. A better choice would be to put a good asset protection plan in place while you are healthy and capable—a modern plan that covers all the bases and isn't some cheap boilerplate document that hasn't been designed for what is happening in our society today.

The remainder of this book is going to talk about what should be included in a modern estate plan. Stay with me. I promise the rest won't be as scary as the first chapter.

"The more things change, the more they stay the same.
~ Jean-Baptiste Alphonse Karr

Chapter 2
Same Old, Same Old

B y now you must be asking yourself: "If society has changed so much, people are living longer, and more people are running into the issues mentioned in Chapter 1, then why haven't all estate planning documents kept up with the times, and why don't all attorneys know these things?"

Three reasons:

1. Taxes
2. Medical science
3. The nature of the legal industry

Taxes

Almost every one of my clients is concerned about taxes eating up their children's inheritance at their deaths, yet almost none of them need to be concerned about taxes.

Benjamin Franklin's old adage "There are two things you can't escape: death and taxes" is no longer true in the United States.

Not long ago, most middle-class Americans *did* need to be concerned about estate or "death taxes." However, over the last decade, the estate tax has essentially been eliminated for most Americans. As recently as the year 2000, every American had to pay a 55 percent tax based on the size of the estate they left at their death. In 2000 if you had an estate of greater than $675,000 you would pay 55 percent on the amount of the estate over $675,000. In other words, if you had a million-dollar estate in the year 2000, your children (or other non-spouse heirs; there is no estate tax between spouses) would pay an estate tax of $178,750 to the Internal Revenue Service within nine months of your death.

One simple planning device most married people did in their estate plans was to combine the estate tax exemption for each spouse in a trust (called an A/B trust). What the A/B trust did was preserve the estate tax credit of the deceased spouse and "pass it along" to the surviving spouse so that, when the surviving spouse died later, the children could use both of their parents' estate tax credits in the estate so there would be less or no tax.

For example, if the estate tax credit in 2000 was $675,000 per person, the two spouses could combine their credits for a total of $1,350,000. This meant twice as much money could be passed tax-free to the children at the death of the second spouse. (Since there is no estate tax when giving everything to a surviving spouse, there would be no tax at the death of the first spouse, but unless the couple did planning, they would lose one of their tax credits at the death of the first spouse. Therefore, they needed to create an A/B tax trust to preserve the credit of the first spouse to die.)

The reason this is not an issue for most people today is that the estate tax credit per person has risen to $5,450,000 per person. A married couple can combine their exemptions today and pass up to $10,900,000 to their children with *no* estate tax. And under the current law, the married couple does not even have to create an A/B trust to capture the estate tax credits of both spouses.

The estate tax impacts less than two-tenths of 1 percent (0.02%) of Americans, yet most Americans still believe this is something they need to be concerned about. It is hard to shake old beliefs.

Why is the legal profession on top of the tax law change but not necessarily up to speed on incapacity, devastating healthcare costs, and protections for your children and grandchildren?

I believe it is a lack of experience and training, and the nature of the industry itself. Many estate planning lawyers looked at estate planning as a tax issue and a probate issue, and they still do, following the cliché: "If you only have a hammer, everything looks like a nail."

So, the legal industry has responded to the change in the tax law by offering what is called a "disclaimer trust," which is designed to deal with the change in the tax law, but does nothing to address the issues of lawsuits, devastating healthcare costs, remarriages, divorces, or premature death of your children before their spouse.

Medical Science

Another reason the legal industry has not kept up with the demands of modern society is, in my opinion, the difference between the legal and the medical professions.

Whereas medical science is in a rush toward innovation, mapping the human genome structure and trying to prolong life, the legal industry still has its collective head buried in the last century. We as a profession continue to do what we always did because in the legal industry "bleeding-edge" technology is not necessarily a good thing.

The problem is that most of the estate planning documents out in the marketplace today were designed to avoid estate taxes and death probates—two things that used to be a big deal 50 years ago, but for the most part are simply not that difficult to plan for today. The more difficult planning scenarios for families today are the types I mention in Chapter 1: incapacity, remarriage of a surviving spouse, and protecting inheritances for the children. Unfortunately, the types of provisions that need to be in a modern estate plan are often exactly the opposite of what is in the traditional "death and tax document" plans that are still prevalent in the marketplace today.

For example, 100 years ago when the average life span was less than 50, few people had to be concerned with long periods of incapacity after an accident or stroke. Usually if you had a stroke you died immediately if not shortly thereafter (unlike Terri Schiavo). Consequently, very little thought was put into protecting people from long-term nursing home costs.

Additionally, 100 years ago people didn't necessarily go to a nursing home. The American family was much less diverse and children tended to stay closer to home, with a traditional working husband

and stay-at-home wife. This meant when one of the parents became ill, there was a caregiver available to take care of them. Today, however, both spouses are often working, and even if one is available, people can't replicate in their homes the medical technology that is available today to care for an elder parent.

That brings us to the final reason estate planning has not kept up with modern society:

The Nature of the Legal Industry

The legal profession is a very conservative profession and slow to change. Attorneys often use prior documents as a template, and unless they have specific experience they don't change their documents.

Also, 100 years ago people didn't live as long, so there were fewer remarriages after one spouse died (because there simply wasn't time). Now with surviving spouses living into their 80s or 90s and remarrying there are consequences on the combined estates and children from prior marriages.

And of course, even as recent as 40 or 50 years ago, divorce was significantly less prevalent as it is today. Parents didn't think their kids were going to get divorced because it was unusual.

The estate planning industry must be extremely confusing to the average consumer, no matter how intelligent he or she is. That's because any attorney can do "estate planning," and can create wills, trusts, and powers of attorney. They aren't required to have a certain amount of experience; they can choose to just create the documents and not help the family after death or incapacity (provide estate administration), or they can concentrate on the court procedure called probate, where they can charge higher fees and spend less time on counseling and planning to avoid probate.

The attorney might do many other things besides estate planning. He or she could cover divorces, business law, and civil litigation. In fact, the estate planning may be a relatively small percentage of overall activities and may be a way to supplement incomes between his or her other types of practice.

I see many attorneys like this. They have a legal software collection that includes software for wills and trusts and they took a course or two in law school, so they have a legal right to do the planning for your family.

Thus, their experience in this area may be limited. Even if they have been practicing law for years they may have created few estate plans. If they have only created a few estate plans, they probably have almost no experience helping families with estate administration issues. Estate administration is the process of helping the family with incapacity issues, planning for devastating nursing home costs, making sure the beneficiaries are protected, etc.

In my opinion, estate administration is one of the most important elements when choosing an estate planning attorney, yet hardly any consumers understand what it is or how it works.

Estate or trust administration is the work that must be done if you or your family has a problem, whether the issue is incapacity, devastating medical or nursing home costs, divorce, or the illness or death of a child or grandchild. A good trust or estate attorney can help you or your family through the legal issues that, if not navigated properly, could end up costing thousands or even millions of dollars (depending on the size of the estate).

Beware the Boilerplate Document

Consumers don't deal with the issues every day so they don't know they need an experienced attorney. They don't know how to measure experience and often select an estate planning attorney based solely on the up-front costs of creating estate planning documents.

Bear in mind, however, that anyone can plug your name into a template and spit out what looks like an impressive estate plan. Unfortunately, you may never find out what a bad bargain you made if your family must deal with the consequences.

The internet has also made estate planning confusing for consumers. Now you can buy a will or trust over the web for almost nothing. In the end, you get what you pay for. There is no experienced professional to help you understand how to build in the protections I am going to show you. The documents are usually the traditional "death documents" I mentioned earlier, and of course when your family has to actually use the them there is no one to call to help when needed. It really is the height of folly to shop for bargains when you don't understand what you're purchasing.

This is why you can buy a "cheap" trust almost anywhere and why people call my office asking only "How much for a trust?"
It would be like buying a car if you had never seen a car before or knew anything about the various models. A couple of decades ago there was a new Yugoslavian car introduced in the United States called the "Yugo." It was very inexpensive. It only cost a few thousand dollars. It was much less expensive than a Toyota or a Honda, or any other known brand.

Imagine you had never owned a car before or even seen one, and had only read about them. They all did the same thing; they had four wheels, a steering wheel, an engine and a drive train. The only difference you could see, since you had no experience, was the price. The Toyota was $20,000 and the Yugo was $5,000. Seems like an easy decision, doesn't it? Why would anyone pay more for the same thing? Congratulations—you are the proud owner of a Yugo. It doesn't work, it caught on fire, and there is no dealer network to get service or warranty, but what a deal you got up-front!

The above are examples of how consumers are taken advantage of in the estate planning marketplace every day. If you want to know why estate planning is an even more likely place to rip off consumers, imagine in the above scenario, that someone could sell you the Yugo and pocket the money, but you didn't take delivery of the car for 20 years. When the car arrives 20 years from now, you're dead, your family crashed in the unsafe vehicle, and the guy who sold it to you is long gone. That's the estate planning marketplace today. In the words of Yakoff Smirnoff: "What a country!"

Experience Needed

In my opinion, the most important thing you can look for when choosing an estate planning attorney is both experience with designing estate plans and experience with estate or trust administration, not necessarily experience with the probate court (which is not where you want your family to end up).

I recently had clients come to me after having the plan that I prepared for them reviewed by another attorney they knew personally and was an old family friend. This attorney told them they didn't "need" a key provision I put in my trusts called a trust protector provision. This provision is specifically designed to keep you and your family out of court if certain circumstances change in either the law or your family circumstances. This attorney had told them they didn't "need" that provision because if things changed he could go to court and get the changes made under the supervision of a judge.

Can you believe this? An attorney counseling a client to remove a provision that could save the family thousands of dollars in attorney fees, not to mention the humiliation and delay of the court proceedings. I suppose the attorney didn't mind going to court since it wouldn't be expensive or humiliating for him. (In fact, it would be quite lucrative for him.) There was *no* upside in removing the provision, but plenty of downside. Needless to say, my clients were happy to keep their estate plan the way it was and learned that not all attorneys understand that most families would rather stay out of court.

An important question to ask is their specific experience in both in designing and implementing the plans. How many families have they worked with during the estate or trust administration process? I believe if an attorney doesn't have experience with trust or estate administration, he or she will have a tough time understanding what can go wrong if the plan isn't properly created in the first place.

After all, how much faith would you have in a winemaker who wouldn't sample his own wine?

Firm Size

My firm has guided over 5,000 families in the design, creation, and implementation of their estate plans, and I've personally advised hundreds of clients when they needed to use them. My office and practice is designed to help families when needed, so even if I'm unavailable my partners, associates and staff will continue to be there for your family. It is important any attorney you select has a continuity plan for your family. Who is going to be there when help is needed, and is it someone you feel comfortable trusting? Despite the efforts of some to depersonalize the process, to me estate planning is the most personal type of law practice. If done properly, it isn't a one-time transaction. This is a relationship that may last decades. You need to feel comfortable that what you are putting in place today is going to be kept up-to-date, and that someone is there for your family to make sure it actually works when needed. You may like that solo practitioner who gives you a good "deal" because they have a small or no staff, but what happens when you are your family needs help and no one is around?

Recap

Now that we've discussed how the trends of estate planning are not necessarily keeping up with the times, what can you do to make sure your plan is up-to-date?

In the Introduction I disclosed the three biggest enemies of your estate:

- **Devastating healthcare costs**
- **Remarriages**
- **Children divorcing or dying before their spouse**

But what can you do about it? If people are living longer and having more "old age" illnesses or periods of incapacity even at younger ages, isn't that just the way it is? What does an estate plan have to do with any of this?

If your wife or husband remarries after your death and decides to give away everything you've both worked for all of your lives to a new spouse's kids, what can you do about it?

Of course, we've all heard: "You can't control from beyond the grave." So, if you leave everything to your children and they lose it in a divorce, and it doesn't end up going to your grandchildren, then so be it. We can't protect our kids forever, right?

Wrong. I'm not talking about controlling from beyond the grave. I'm talking about easy commonsense planning that protects you, your spouse, your children, and your grandchildren (even if you don't have grandchildren yet) from the common, everyday occurrences that happen in families and can collectively cost millions if not billions of dollars in unnecessary losses—losses due to devastating healthcare costs, remarriages of a surviving spouse without protections for the estate, and leaving inheritances to children so they are exposed to divorces, taxes, and potential creditors.

The rest of this book will show you the ways to protect your family from the three biggest enemies it may face in the coming decades. This book will help you design a modern asset protection plan.

Section II
Healthcare Planning

"History is a race between education and catastrophe."
~ H.G. Wells

Chapter 3
What Every Family Must Know

Required Reading

If you don't read any other chapter in this book, you must read this chapter and the one that follows. After you've finished, if you're married, make sure your spouse reads it, and if you have adult children, make sure they read it. The information in the next two chapters could literally keep you and your family from going broke, yet I have found that very few people are aware of the options that could save then hundreds of thousands of dollars in unnecessary expense!

It is important that other members of your family are aware of these planning options because you never know who may have to institute planning for whom in your family. If you are the *only* one who knows your options and you are the one that needs help, no one else in your family will know what to do. Please encourage your other family members to at least be aware that there are steps you can take now to protect yourself will put you miles ahead of most people in these situations.

What is this horrible evil of which you and your family need to be so well informed?

Well, as you probably already know by now, it is the devastating costs of healthcare for one or both parents. Since people are living longer there is a higher likelihood that our minds and bodies will break down as we age.

In addition, the concept of the nuclear family, where everyone lived in the same town and the kids lived a few miles away, has been gone for decades. In today's modern family children may move across the continent or across the world. Whereas 75 years ago a son went to work and a daughter stayed home as a caregiver, now both your son and your daughter will be working and there is no one to stay home for dear old Mom or Dad.

This change in the nature of our society has led to the increase in retirement communities, assisted living facilities, and nursing homes. No one likes to think about it, but the fact is that once you hit 65, you have a 40-percent probability of spending some time in a nursing facility before you die.

In fact, the above statistic may be a little low. According to Muriel Gillick's recent book, *The Denial of Aging*: "The latest prediction is that if you are just now turning 65, you have nearly a 50 percent chance of spending some time in a nursing home before you die. Approximately 10 percent of those nursing home stays will be short-term, intended for recuperation after a hospitalization. The remainder will be for the long haul, with discharge to a funeral parlor, not to the family home."

The growth in the number and proportion of older adults is unprecedented in the history of the United States. Two factors—longer life spans and aging Baby Boomers—will combine to double the population of Americans aged 65 and older during the next 25 years. By 2030, there will be 71 million American older adults, accounting for roughly 20 percent of the U.S. population.

And as the proportion of us reaching 65 increases, the cost of providing healthcare for an older American is three to five times greater than the cost for someone younger than 65. As a result, by 2030, the nation's healthcare spending is projected to increase by 25 percent.

Medicare spending has grown about nine-fold in the past two decades, from $37 billion in 1980 to $336 billion in 2005 (according to the Center for Disease Control's "The State of Aging and Health in America," 2007).

The Medicare Gap!

The problem is that Medicare spending, even though it is increasing to cover the increased costs of many illnesses, does not cover certain illnesses at all. Many Americans are under the false and dangerous assumption that the costs of their healthcare once they reach age 65 will be covered by Medicare. *Not true!* The chart below shows the illnesses (in light gray) that are typically covered by Medicare and the illnesses (in dark gray) that are likely to break the family bank because the long-term care that is often required by these illnesses is *not* covered by Medicare.

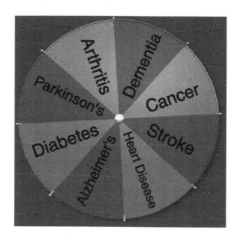

Medicare does provide some coverage for long-term care in the event you or a family member contracts one of the diseases in red above. However, the costs that Medicare will cover are extremely limited. Medicare will only pay for up to 100 days in a skilled nursing facility, and then after that you are on your own. For example, if you had a stroke and needed long-term convalescent care either at home or in a nursing facility, the costs for such care would *not* be covered by Medicare.

Who Pays?

Who would cover the costs of care in such a circumstance? Well, if you were fortunate enough to have purchased long-term care insurance, then it may pay for a portion or even all of the care. If you don't have long-term care insurance, then you would pay out of your pocket until such time that you were sufficiently impoverished so that you could qualify for assistance under another government program called Medicaid (Medi-Cal in California).

Medicaid is a combined federal and state program that will pay for some of the healthcare costs of the poor. That's right: you have to be poor with a maximum allowable income and/or assets to qualify for assistance under Medicaid.

This means in a scenario where you or a spouse have a stroke and the ill spouse needs long-term care, you wouldn't qualify under Medicaid (in most states) until you have spent down your assets so that the spouse with the stroke has only $2,000 left of non-exempt assets. (I will explain non-exempt assets later in this chapter.) The well spouse can have no more than $120,900 left (known as the Community Spouse Resource Allowance, or CSRA for 2017). If you are single, then you can have no more than $2,000 of non-exempt assets.

As you can see, unless you have long-term care insurance, you basically have to go broke before there is a government insurance plan to pay for your care. Notice, however, that if you had three heart attacks, two multiple by-pass surgeries, and the associated hospital stays associated with the heart attacks and surgeries, the majority of your costs would be covered under Medicare.

Similarly, if you contract cancer, Medicare will pay for the majority of your care, but if you have Parkinson's, Medicare will only pay for doctor visits and drug treatments. The expensive in-home or nursing home care that will be needed is all on you or your family.

Clearly, the current state of healthcare coverage in the United States is a gamble. If you leave your families' healthcare in the hands of the government, you will be dependent upon what they believe should be covered and what shouldn't. As stated earlier, the increasing numbers of Americans who are going to be over age 65 means the exact kinds of diseases that are occurring more and more frequently in the population are the illnesses that are *not* currently covered under Medicare.

You may not be able to do anything about the costs of healthcare to the nation, but you *can* do something to protect your family from devastating increases in cost that are the result of *uncovered* healthcare expenses.

What can you do? Let's examine the options for paying the uncovered healthcare costs identified above. How can you make sure you are covered as much as possible, with minimum exposure to yourself and your family?

The first thing you can do is look into obtaining long-term care insurance (LTCI). LTCI is insurance designed to cover the costs of in-home care, assisted living, and nursing home costs if needed.

Long-Term Care Insurance Traps!

Here are just a few basic facts about long-term care insurance so you will know what to look for when shopping:

1. Make sure of the quality and rating of the insurance company issuing the policy. Do not purchase a long-term care policy from an insurance company you are not familiar with and that does not have a long history of being financially sound with proven reserves. Your policy is only as good as the company issuing it, and if it goes broke, there are limited state programs that will guarantee only a small portion of your policy, if at all.

2. Read the fine print, or better yet have your attorney review the policy before signing. Make sure the policy provides 100 percent of benefits whether the care is provided in your home, in assisted living, or in a nursing home. Some policies provide limited benefits for in-home care or assisted living and only pay 100 percent of the stated benefits if the person is in a nursing home. This is exactly

the opposite of what most people want. They would rather have care provided in their home. Unfortunately, some insurance companies trim the premiums down to make the policy look good by offering coverage in only the nursing home scenario and limited or no coverage for in-home care. I have seen more than one consumer not realize this until it was too late.

3. Make sure of the maximum lifetime benefits amount is payable under the policy. For example, many policies state on the cover page that they will pay up to $6,000 per month or $200 per day which sounds pretty reasonable. What they don't tell you is that page 11 of the policy states that the monthly and daily amounts of coverage are limited by a lifetime maximum of $150,000 or $200,000. In today's world of $10,000/month for nursing home care, $150,000 is just a year and three months.

4. Be aware of inflation coverage. Most long-term care policies sold today have an inflation rider, which means the stated benefits will go up every year by some percentage to allow for inflation. The amount I see most often is 5 percent per year. Once again you must be aware of the lifetime maximum amount in the policy. Does that also go up every year by the same amount? Common sense would say yes, but these policies are regulated by each state. Your state may not be quite as consumer friendly as another state, so make sure that both the stated daily, monthly, and lifetime benefits are covered by the inflation rider with the costs of long-term care going up exponentially.

5. Beware of group long-term care policies offered through your employer. Many people are confused about long-term care insurance. They often tell me that they think they are covered through their employer. The minute they say they *think* they are covered, I know they aren't. Group health insurance policies do not typically cover long-term care expenses. Occasionally some private employers and

government agencies do offer long-term policies to their employees as an optional benefit, but if they do they are clearly identified as additions to your regular healthcare coverage. These policies are always optional and not a part of your group health plan, and they require an additional premium. Additionally, you will be issued separate policy paperwork and there is *no way* you would not be aware that you have this benefit.

Let's assume, however, that you are one of the few people who does have long-term care insurance through your employer. Then you should be on high alert! Why? Because almost every long-term care policy offered as part of a group plan through an employer has been dangerously stripped of its benefits.

In other words, the employer gets a really basic, cheap plan simply to offer an added benefit that its competitors do not. When I look at the benefits of these polices, they are usually far inferior to what is offered in the private marketplace. For example, the lifetime maximum benefits hidden on page 11 are usually much lower than individual policies.

I especially see this with the plans offered to government employees. In California there was recent outrage when the premiums on state workers' long-term care policies went up by as much as 60 percent in one year. This would *not* have happened in a private policy, but the state got a really good deal on the insurance policies by opting out of some of the protections afforded to consumers who were not state workers!

The bottom line is: if you are considering purchasing a long-term care policy, be sure to have it reviewed by an estate planning or elder law attorney with some experience in this area. I am happy to review policies for my clients before they purchase them and have often helped them get much better terms.

What if Insurance Is Not an Option?

For many people, long-term care insurance is not an option. Like all insurance, it is only reasonably priced when the insurance companies don't think you will use it. If you are older you may not be able to afford the high premiums, or in many cases you may not be eligible for coverage because of a pre-existing condition.

Even if you do have coverage or can afford to purchase it, however, you should not depend on your long-term care insurance coverage as the complete solution to paying for devastating healthcare expenses.

The reasons you can't depend on long-term care insurance exclusively are many. I have summarized just a few of them below.

1. Even with the best policies your coverage will be limited and would not fully cover you or a loved for a truly catastrophic illness. For example, if you or a loved one gets Alzheimer's or Parkinson's these illnesses can require care that will outlive your long-term care coverage. Long-term care policies are typically for three years but sometimes even less.

2. Your long-term care coverage will not cover all your expenses. Right now, the average monthly cost of a nursing home in my area is between $9,000 and $10,000 per month. This does not include special care for Alzheimer's patients. It is unheard of for long-term care benefits to cover anywhere near that amount. Even with an inflation rider, the insured would be fortunate to be receiving $4,000 to $5,000 per month to go against the actual costs. The policy benefits are not keeping up with the nursing home costs, which means the difference of $4,000 to $5,000 per month is being paid by your family. If you have a well spouse at home that means they need to pay the nursing home expenses and their monthly living expenses as well. So, for example, even if someone had long-term care insurance the spouse living at home would need to come up with $5,000/month for the nursing home, plus whatever the monthly expenses are for the well spouse living at home. If the monthly expenses are, say $3,000, that means they

need to come up with $8,000/month—or $96,000/year (after taxes)—just to live. This doesn't allow for vacations, new cars, or other unforeseen expenses (like a new roof on the house).

3. The premium costs for maintaining long-term care policies may become prohibitive even for a policy you already own. Insurance companies like to say that they can't raise rates for individual long-term care insurance policy holders, that they can only raise rates for an entire class, and that this therefore protects the individual consumer. What most consumers don't know, however, is that the regulatory body that determines whether an insurance company can raise rates is the insurance commission of each state. These commissions will not deny a rate increase to an insurance company if it shows an increase in costs. With the rising claims being made to insurance companies for their long-term care policies, they have no problem justifying rate increases to consumers. If you think the premiums you are paying today will remain the same for the life of your policy, you may be sadly disappointed. There may come a time (perhaps right before you most need it) when you simply can no longer afford the policy.

Now that you know the limitations of Medicare, group health insurance through your employer, and long-term care policies in general, is there any other way to make sure your family will not have to go broke in the event of a devastating illness? The good news is that yes, there is a way, and I am going to explain it in the last part of this chapter. Before I do that, however, I want to take a minute to address the federal healthcare law that went into effect in 2014, the Patient Protection and Affordable Care Act (commonly referred to as Obamacare).

Many people are under the mistaken impression that Obamacare will solve the issues I have just discussed because the law states that insurance companies can now no longer limit the lifetime maximums of their coverage. Please don't make the mistake of thinking the law applies to long-term care insurance policies. It does *not!* I am very familiar with the law and teach continuing education courses on the new law to the financial community. The law does indeed prevent insurance companies from cutting off your health insurance if your care becomes too expensive. The law, however, does nothing to prevent the lifetime maximums or benefit gaps under long-term care insurance. The law also does not require an employer to offer long-term care insurance as part of your coverage.

This is not a political book, and I am not a politician. I am not here to say the new law is good or bad. I think it does address some glaring holes in the health insurance industry, but unfortunately the types of illnesses and costs I have outlined above are not resolved or even adequately addressed by the Patient Protection and Affordable Care Act. Again, one of the reasons these illnesses have such a devastating impact on families is that so many people are unprepared for them. They think they are covered and they are not. Don't make the mistake of thinking the government is going to fix this problem for you.

What About Medicaid?

Okay, so if it's up to us, what can we do? As I mentioned earlier in this chapter, there is a government program that will pay for the long-term care expenses of Americans called Medicaid. You may remember, that I said you really had to be broke to qualify for Medicaid. In other words, Medicaid rules state that to be eligible for assistance, you can't have too much money or other assets. I left out an important detail, because Medicaid doesn't require you to be broke; it only states you can't have too much of certain types of assets (also known as non-exempt assets). On the other hand, Medicaid rules don't care how much of another type of asset you may have, known as exempt assets.

Before I outline some of the Medicaid rules I want to take just a minute to talk about what Medicaid is and how it is administered.

Medicaid is a means-tested entitlement program that finances the delivery of primary and acute medical services as well as long-term care services and supports. Medicaid is a federal and state partnership that is jointly financed by the federal government and the states.

There is a set of federal laws for the administration of Medicaid funds. However, the states can modify these laws and rules somewhat if they are willing to absorb the additional costs. The Medicaid program is administered by the states, not the federal government, so there are differences among the states as to how Medicaid is applied for, granted, and administered.

Beware Across State Lines!

Be careful if you live in Ohio and your aunt in Indiana gives you advice on how to qualify for Medicaid. The rules are different among the states, and you will need a qualified attorney to make sure you do not violate the rules if you are attempting to qualify by employing some of the tactics mentioned in this book.

In California, for instance, there are legal ways to gift assets out of your name to a loved one so you can qualify for Medicaid without having to spend all your assets down to the prescribed levels ($2,000 for an individual and $120,900 for a well spouse). This method is not available in other states and may not be available in California for long.

Also, some states look at both your income and assets to determine if you qualify for Medicaid, whereas other states (like California) only look at your assets.

The state agency in charge of administering the program is the state Department of Health Services. This department is responsible for reviewing and approving or rejecting applications, and for recovering assets from your estate (if there are any) to reimburse the state for expenditures made on your behalf.

Your State Wants Your Estate!

That's right! Unlike Medicare, where the federal government does not take your home or bank account to recover the amount of money spent on your healthcare costs, the Medicaid program in each state has an estate recovery department in charge of getting money from your estate (or your family if transfers were made in violation of the rules) for expenses it has paid on your behalf.

Therefore, it is important to note that there are two parts to Medicaid planning: One part is to reposition assets so you can qualify without having to spend all your resources, and the other part is to plan in such a way that the state can't take your assets at your death.

Medicaid Planning 101

Before I provide some examples of how to use Medicaid to pay for devastating long-term care expenses, let me first give my typical attorney's disclaimer: The examples and rules I am using in this book are for illustrative purposes only. I am using examples based on the Medicaid rules in California; the rules may be different in your state and for your unique situation. In addition, the rules may have changed since the writing of this book, and there is no guarantee that any examples used herein will be effective for your situation. You should consult with an experienced attorney in this area before attempting any asset transfers or any other type of Medicaid planning.

With that out of the way let me give you an example of how someone could use Medicaid to help pay for his or her long-term care expenses. In our example, I am going to use California rules, which may not apply in another state. I am also going to use a hypothetical example based upon a number of cases I have worked on over the years.

Let us say Bob and Sally are a married couple in California. Bob is 68 and Sally is 66. They have two adult children (Jill and Jack). Bob and Sally have the following assets:

1. Home, worth $700,000 (no mortgage)
2. Bob's IRA, worth $350,000

3. Joint brokerage account, worth $80,000
4. Joint savings account, worth $25,000
5. 2004 Buick, worth $14,000
6. Personal household goods

They also have the following monthly income:

1. Bob's pension: $1,500
2. Bob's Social Security: $2,000
3. Sally's Social Security: $1,000

Let us assume that Bob and Sally were responsible citizens and a few years ago they went to a friend of theirs who was an estate planning attorney and had a revocable trust, financial powers of attorney, and healthcare powers of attorney prepared.

The documents stated that Bob and Sally were the trustees (or managers) of their trust while they were alive and capable, but that if one of them were incapacitated or dead the remaining spouse would be in charge by themselves. The documents also said if the remaining parent were incapacitated or dead, the adult children could serve as trustees.

The documents were traditional probate avoidance and death documents (which are still the predominant types of estate planning documents used today), and they said nothing about allowing for planning for Medicaid or government assistance.

What happens when Bob has a stroke? If Bob's stroke is serious, he may be incapacitated for quite some time. In fact, he may not be able to talk, sign his name, or communicate with Sally or anyone else. Once the doctors tell Sally that he needs convalescent care he will no longer be eligible for Medicare, and she must either take him home or put him in a nursing home. Either way, she will not be able to care for Bob herself, because he needs 24/7 care. She would need someone to relieve her while she sleeps, and even when she is awake she is unable to physically lift him Bob and provide the level of care necessary for him to survive, let alone recover and improve.

If Sally moves Bob to a nursing home where they have the facilities to provide the care he needs, it will cost her roughly $9,000 per month. From the above list, you can see that Bob and Sally's monthly income is only $4,500 per month. Bob and Sally's average normal monthly household expenses are $4,000/month before the nursing home, so that only leaves and extra $500/month for the nursing home, which means Sally will have to come up with an extra $8,500 per month to pay the nursing home costs.

Where will Sally get the additional $8,500 per month? Bob and Sally have $80,000 in a brokerage account and $25,000 in savings, for a combined total of $105,000. This will last her a little over 12 months ($105,000/8,500= 12.35 months).

Sally may have to take money out of Bob's retirement account, or perhaps she can take out a mortgage on the house. However, when Sally calls the financial institution where Bob keeps his IRA she finds out that they will not give her access to the funds. Even though she has a power of attorney that says she can control Bob's financial accounts in the event of his incapacity, the financial institution has a company policy that it will not honor powers of attorney that executed over two years ago. Sally is shocked to find this out, and she goes to her attorney to see if he can help her. He tells her that many institutions have this policy to protect themselves from people trying to use old, out-of-date powers of attorney. He tells Sally, however, that under state law he can compel the financial institution to accept the power of attorney and give her access, but he will have to go to court and get a judge to order the company to do so. That will take time and more money that Sally doesn't have.

Sally then tries to get a home equity line on her house, but the mortgage officer tells her that she will need Bob's signature for the home equity loan since the trust requires both parties to sign for a mortgage. Sally is confused by this, and she goes back to her attorney. He explains that even though there is language in the document that says she is in charge during an incapacity, the document does not allow one trustee to take on debt without the consent of the other spouse, and that the document was designed so that a well spouse could pay bills but not change the estate plan of an ill spouse. After all, we wouldn't want a spouse to take advantage of an ill spouse while he or she was incapacitated, would we? (This is what traditional estate planning documents were concerned with, not the need for a well spouse to protect assets or pay for long-term care.)

Again, Sally's attorney can get this resolved with a court proceeding known as a conservatorship. It shouldn't take more than six months and $15,000, according to her attorney. Surprisingly, her attorney doesn't seem the least bit bothered that everything has to go back to court, even though he initially assured Bob and Sally that their estate plan would keep them out of court.

Of course, Bob and Sally's attorney will make substantially more going to court than he did drawing up their plan in the first place. It is true that some attorneys like to do low-cost estate plans so they can build a business of clients that will provide them with a lucrative revenue stream when they need to use them. This is another example of why you should never buy a trust based on its up-front cost.

Must Have Medicaid Triggers!

Not only do Bob and Sally's documents not allow Sally to have full control of her and Bob's assets, but they also lack something that is even more important in this situation: **Medicaid Triggers**. I will explain Medicaid Triggers more fully in the next chapter, but at this point it's important to know that unless Sally has this important language in all of her documents, she will be unable to do Medicaid planning without going back to court and seeking the court's permission, which is time consuming and expensive. *If her estate planning attorney had included these important provisions in her estate plan, she would now be able to qualify Bob for Medicaid without having to spend all their money and going broke first!*

You might be asking at this point how Medicaid could be an option since Bob and Sally seem to have too many assets and too much income. However, when I said earlier that Bob could only have $2,000 worth of assets and Sally could only have $120,900 of assets, I also said that was the amount of non-exempt assets they could have. For the purposes of qualifying for Medicaid, the state divides your assets into two categories: non-exempt and exempt. While it is true that an individual can only have $2,000 of non-exempt assets and a well spouse can only have $120,900 of non-exempt assets, you can have as much money in exempt assets as you want.

Exempt Assets Don't Count

The following are examples of non-exempt and exempt assets:

Non-Exempt	Exempt
Your home	Your home
Retirement accounts	Retirement accounts
Savings accounts	Medicaid qualified annuities
Brokerage accounts	Medicaid trusts
Certificates of deposit	Unavailable investment real estate
Available investment real estate	Court-approved increase in the CSRA

I am not going to go over each asset in each category above. I am providing this list to illustrate my point: you can have an unlimited amount of assets if they are on the exempt side of the equation. There are Medicaid trusts, Medicaid qualified annuities, and ways to make investment real estate unavailable that an attorney can explain further. I am providing just a partial list of some of the tools at my disposal to protect families' assets. If needed, we can use these and others to make sure your family doesn't have to go broke to pay for long-term care expenses.

The above list is confusing because I show both the home and retirement accounts as both non-exempt and exempt assets. How can they be both? Because the status can be changed. For example, the home is usually exempt as long as you state on the Medicaid application that the person going into the nursing home has the intent to return home. If you state that he or she does not have an intent to return home, the home will not be exempt. Also note that even though the home can be exempt for the purpose of qualifying for Medicaid, if the home remains in the name of the person in a nursing home and is in that person's name when he or she dies, the state will be able to place a lien on the home to recover the amount of money it paid to the nursing home in Medicaid benefits.

A retirement account is also not always an exempt asset, but it can become exempt. For example, if the owner of the retirement account has not yet begun receiving his or her required minimum distributions because he or she is not yet 70 1/2 years old then the retirement account will not be exempt. However, a retirement account can be exempt and will not count against you for the purposes of qualifying for Medicaid if you begin a minimum required distribution. So, for example, in Bob and Sally's case, Bob has a $350,000 IRA and has not yet started taking his Required Minimum Distributions (RMDs), so he would have too much money to qualify for Medicaid. However, if Sally had the proper authorizing documents that would allow her to begin taking out a minimum amount from the IRA, the entire amount would move from the non-exempt category to the exempt asset category, and Bob would become eligible for Medicaid without having to spend down all of his retirement account. This also would not count against Sally's $120,900 CSRA, so she could have the $350,000 plus another $120,900 of non-exempt assets.

Medicaid planning is the process of legally taking assets in the non-exempt category and moving them into the exempt category. There are a number of strategies and tactics that can be employed so that people do not have to spend all their assets down to zero before they can qualify for government assistance.

Beware of the Look-Back Period

There is something called the "look-back" period for the purposes of Medicaid planning, and sometimes this leads to confusion as to what planning can be done. There are a number of months where the Department of Health Services wants to see all financial transactions prior to your application for Medicaid. As of this writing, in California it is 30 months, but in most states it is 60 months. (The California rule may have changed by the time you are reading this.)

The look-back period means that if you made a non-exempt transfer of any of your assets within the look-back period you will be disqualified from receiving Medicaid benefits for the period of time that those assets could have been used to pay for your care. *Bear in mind, however, that there is no look-back period for transfers of exempt assets such as a home.* So you could transfer a home within the look-back period and not trigger a period of ineligibility. (However, there are other considerations such as capital gains tax and property tax you must be aware of. Never attempt this without the help of a qualified attorney.)

For example, let's say in the above example Sally gave a gift of their $80,000 brokerage account to her daughter 12 months before she applied for Medicaid. On her application Sally has to show bank records and disclose the gift. If she doesn't disclose this information, she may be eligible for free room and board at the state prison.

What happens when Sally does disclose the gift? She will be disqualified from receiving Medicaid for the number of months that the money could have been used to pay for Bob's care. The disqualification period is calculated as follows:

Amount of gift within look-back period = $80,000
Monthly amount Medicaid pays nursing home if you qualified = $5,800 (rounded)
$80,000 divided by $5,800 = 14 months of ineligibility (rounded)

This means that she would be disqualified from receiving Medicaid benefits for 14 months, which is the number of months that her money would have paid for care (based on the state reimbursement rate, not the actual nursing home rate).

This doesn't mean you go to jail for making the gift or that you can never receive Medicaid. It only means you can't receive Medicaid until your period of ineligibility is up.

Let's look at a way someone could use this to their advantage. Let's say that Bob and Sally had $500,000 in a brokerage account, and Sally didn't want to have to spend all the money to pay for Bob's nursing home costs. She could give $250,000 to her children with the understanding they would hold it for her and Bob. If Sally did this, she would be disqualified from receiving benefits for approximately 43 months ($250,000/$5,800 = 43.10).

The "Half a Loaf" Strategy

How would Sally pay for the 43 months? She would use the $250,000 that she didn't give away to pay for Bob's care. This $250,000 would pay for his care for the period of disqualification, and the $250,000 that was gifted to her children would be out of her name and in the name of her children, so it would no longer count against Bob and Sally for the purposes of qualifying for Medicaid.

Don't Try This on Your Own!

A word of caution! These are simplified examples to illustrate that there are many options available to pay for long-term care. However, the tactics I have mentioned here are not necessarily the ones I would recommend for your unique circumstances. There are even better strategies than the ones I have described; I gave you some of the simplest ones to illustrate a point. With advance planning and the proper documents in your estate plan, you do not have to go broke to pay for long-term care. It is not always a good idea to make outright gifts to children, as they may lose your money. There are many other ways to plan so please do not run out and try and do this on your own!

There is one more very important point about Medicaid you should know about. If you are a private pay patient to a nursing home, you will pay much more than the state reimbursement rate. In Bob and

Sally's case the private pay rate is $9,000/month and the state reimburses the nursing home for $5,800. What happens to the difference? Are Bob and Sally obligated to pay the difference? Absolutely not! The nursing home has to eat the difference. This is important to remember, because for this reason alone it makes sense to qualify for Medicaid so Bob and Sally can get the monthly bill reduced.

Don't Forget Your Share of Cost

Do know, however, that even though Bob and Sally may be able to move assets around so they qualify for Medicaid, the state may still want a share of their monthly income to help defray the costs being paid by the state.

For example, the state will want a portion of Bob's income to help pay the cost. This is known as the share of cost, or soc. In the case of Bob and Sally, who have a $4,500/month income, will the state take all of this? No. The state will let Sally keep income that is in her name alone (like social security, retirement account distributions, pensions etc.), but it will take Bob's income to help defray the cost. The good news, however, is that Sally is able to keep some of Bob's income. This amount is known as the minimum monthly needs allowance, or MMNA. At the time of this writing Sally is allowed to keep a minimum of $3,023 of income. She is entitled to have more than this if it is her separate income (say a pension or large retirement account), but if she doesn't have at least $3,023 per month in income she is allowed to keep some of Bob's income to get her income up to the minimum. In this example, Bob has $3,500/month in income ($1,500 pension and $2,000 in social security), and Sally only has $1,000 from her social security. Sally will keep $2,023 of the $3,500, and the difference of $1,477 per month will be taken by the state as share of cost. Again, just to be clear, if Sally had $5,000 of her own separate income that was not joint income, she would be entitled to keep the full $5,000 but she would not be entitled to any of Bob's income.

Why Have Long-Term Care Insurance?

What if Bob and Sally had long-term care insurance and it was paying $4,000/month toward Bob's $8,500/month nursing home bill? Could Bob and Sally still qualify for Medicaid assistance? Yes, and it would work the same way. Once we did Medicaid planning and moved assets around so that Bob had less than $2,000 of non-exempt assets and Sally had less than $120,900 of non-exempt assets, then the state would pick up the difference to the nursing home that the insurance company is not covering.

Sally does not get to keep any more money than her allowed MMNA; the nursing home just makes out better. I know what you are saying at this point: "If long-term care insurance doesn't allow me to keep any more money, and under Medicaid the nursing home has to eat the difference, then why should I pay for long-term care insurance? After all, what do I care if the nursing home gets paid its full amount or not?" Good question, but the reason you should still have long-term care insurance if you can afford it is that Medicaid only pays for costs of a nursing home. It does not pay for the types of long-term care you might rather have, such as in-home care or assisted living at a nice retirement community.

A good long-term care insurance policy can pay for 100 percent of the costs of in-home care and for 100 percent of the costs of a good assisted living facility, which is the preferred option for most people. I highly recommend a good-term care insurance policy if you can qualify for and afford it. A good policy combined with a modern, up-to-date estate plan (asset protection plan!) with Medicaid Triggers can provide the total solution to protect you and your family from devastating healthcare expenses that are destroying the peace of mind and family wealth of more and more Americans.

No Medicaid Triggers, No Options

Sally and Bob did not have Medicaid Triggers in their estate planning documents, so all of the various planning options and the ability to move assets from the non-exempt category to the exempt category were just wishful thinking.

I can't tell you how many times people have come to me with traditional estate planning documents and I have had to tell them we must go to court to try to get permission to protect their family's assets. It is hard to understand why documents are prepared that practically force families into the legal quagmire known as the state probate system. I am confident that most estate plans being drafted today are inflexible and rely upon the court system to address changes in the law and in family circumstances.

The probate courts today have as many trust probate cases as those with people who did no planning. Think about that. People went out, paid money, and did their planning trying to avoid the court system, and yet their family ended up in court anyway!

Most of the trusts and estate plans that I have had to take to court could have avoided the court system altogether if only there had been proper counseling, expertise, and experience used in designing the plan in the first place. In the next chapter, I am going explain how to make sure your family has a modern asset protection plan that is designed to avoid the problems created by these traditional estate plans. I will explain why you need certain language in your trusts and powers of attorney, and I will show you exactly what to look for so you won't be taken advantage of like Bob and Sally. With good planning and modern documents, there is no reason anyone in your family should have to beg a judge to let you keep your assets. You and your family will be in charge and in control!

> "Blessed are the hearts that can bend;
> they shall never be broken."
>
> ~ Albert Camus

Chapter 4
The Secret is Flexibility

As alluded to in the first chapter, traditional estate planning was based on trying to avoid expenses for your family at death. The plans were designed to avoid death probates (court procedures to transfer assets to your heirs) and taxes. Traditional trusts and powers of attorneys did not anticipate that the creators of the documents could have long-periods of incapacity, such as Alzheimer's, dementia, or strokes.

That said, here we are in a brave new world of longevity, but attorneys are still pumping out trusts and powers of attorneys that say, essentially: "If you get sick and can't pay your bills, your power-of-attorney or your successor trustee can pay your bills, but they sure as heck can't change anything about your estate plan. They can't change the title on anything you own, they can't change your estate planning documents, and they certainly can't make gifts of your money to other people beyond a very small annual gifting allowance.

This makes sense, right? I mean, after all, we wouldn't want anyone to change our estate plan or give our assets away while we're in a coma or we have Alzheimer's, right? Wrong!

Who Do You Trust?

Do you trust your spouse? Do you trust your children? If you don't trust them to take care of you and look after your interests, why would you make them successor trustees in the first place? The fact of the matter is most people do trust their spouse and their children. Most people thought they were giving them these powers when they created their documents, but their attorneys never really explained their options and told them that they had choices. They simply pulled out the old death documents that were designed to avoid taxes and death probates, and had very little language regarding planning for healthcare expenses.

In fact, most people existing documents are shocked to learn that they don't have these powers in their documents. It is very confusing. In California, for instance, the standard statutory power of attorney warns everyone in bold language "BEWARE BY SIGNING THIS DOCUMENT YOU ARE GIVING YOUR AGENT CONTROL OF YOUR PROPERTY." And yet the California Probate Code Section 4264 also says the following:

> **Section 4264 of the California Probate Code.** An attorney-in-fact under a power of attorney may perform any of the following acts on behalf of the principal or with the property of the principal **only if the power of attorney expressly grants that authority to the attorney-in-fact:**
>
> (a) Create, modify, revoke, or terminate a trust, in whole or in part. If a power of attorney under this division empowers the attorney-in-fact to modify or revoke a trust created by the principal, the trust may be modified or revoked by the attorney-in-fact **only as provided in the trust instrument.**
>
> (b) Fund with the principal's property a trust not created by the principal or a person authorized to create a trust on behalf of the principal.
>
> (c) Make or revoke a gift of the principal's property in trust or otherwise.
>
> (d) Exercise the right to reject, disclaim, release, or consent to a reduction in, or modification of, a share

in, or payment from, an estate, trust, or other fund on behalf of the principal. This subdivision does not limit the attorney-in-fact's authority to disclaim a detrimental transfer to the principal with the approval of the court.

(e) Create or change survivorship interests in the principal's property or in property in which the principal may have an interest.

(f) Designate or change the designation of beneficiaries to receive any property, benefit, or contract right on the principal's death.

(g) Make a loan to the attorney-in-fact.

Traditional Death Documents Don't Work

As you can see from the above excerpt of the California Probate Code, a standard power of attorney does not let someone change your trusts or estate plan unless it has been specifically spelled out in the document. Why would this language be important to have in your documents if your spouse or your children needed to do Medicaid planning for you?

Let's reflect on the example of Sally and Bob from the previous chapter. When Sally went back to see her attorney, she was told she didn't have complete control of her husband's assets, and that her attorney would have to go to court and ask permission to do Medicaid planning. Part of the reason was that she had a statutory power of attorney that did not let her take things out of Bob's name, which is exactly what she needed to do to qualify Bob for Medicaid! She may also need to create a new, special kind of irrevocable Medicaid trust for Bob to protect his assets, but unless the power of attorney specifically has language granting that authority, she won't be able to do it.

There was another reason Sally couldn't modify Bob's plan, however. Their trust was a traditional death document that specifically did *not* allow for modification in the event of incapacity. In order to be able to modify someone's trust, the trust itself has to say it can be modified by someone holding a valid power of attorney, and then the power of attorney has to specifically state that the agent has the authority to amend or revoke that person's trust. You can't do one without the other. *Both* documents must have the proper language and be coordinated to work under state law.

I can't tell you how many times someone has come to me with an existing trust and powers of attorney that say it can only be modified by a power of attorney, but the power of attorney did not have the specific language needed under the probate code to make the changes needed. Unfortunately, the results are the same for the client: a court proceeding a judge is requested to do what the couple thought they had done in the first place!

This doesn't have to be the outcome for your family. With properly drafted documents, your spouse or your adult children can save your wealth from being eaten up by unnecessary healthcare costs and other unforeseen catastrophes. Your documents need to have built-in flexibility that allows them to be modified by the people you love and trust.

By the way, have you noticed how important it is to have your documents consistent with the probate code of the state you live in? Each state has its own probate code, and if your documents are not compliant with your states code, you or your loved ones will not be able to do the type of advanced planning we are talking about.

You may be asking yourself, then, why the internet and the bookstores (and even certain television personalities) tell you that you can buy their documents, fill in the blanks, and they will be "good in all 50 states." Well, that is because when they say "good" they mean they are "good if you die, but not so good if you have a devastating illness, there is a change in the state or federal law, you have a change in circumstances, or if you don't want to lose tens if not hundreds of thousands of dollars in attorney's fees, court costs, and healthcare expenses." That doesn't include the frustration and mental anguish you or your family will go through trying to get things fixed after the fact.

Other than that, these documents may be "good." I'm kidding, of course; they don't really appear to be that "good" at all.

These documents are not compliant with the probate codes in all 50 states. They use generic language that sounds good and looks logical, but doesn't work for the types of asset protection that more and more families will need.

Now back to Bob and Sally. If they had had the language above in their power of attorney, and their trust allowed it to be modified by the power of attorney, would that be enough to allow Sally to do Medicaid planning for Bob? That is not all that is needed. They also need specific language that allows them to do other things possibly necessary for Medicaid planning. This language needs to be throughout the documents, it needs to be clear and unambiguous so there is no doubt of intent, and it must be consistent with state law. These are the Medicaid Triggers that are essential for a modern estate plan.

You May Need an Irrevocable Trust

I briefly mentioned in the previous section that part of asset protection planning may involve setting up and putting your assets in an irrevocable trust. What does that mean? In the definitions section of this book I defined two terms: revocable trust and irrevocable trust. Up till now I have been talking about revocable trusts. Revocable trusts are trusts that can be changed easily and you maintain control of your assets. But what about irrevocable trusts? When would you want one of those, if ever?

The irrevocable trust is basically the opposite of a revocable trust. It is not as easy to change, and you lose control of your assets. Why would you want that? The rule to remember is: what you can get, a creditor can get. So, if I want to protect my assets I may want to give them away. I know at this point you are saying that makes no sense. But if I said you can give assets to an irrevocable trust and still use them during your lifetime it might start to make more sense, right?

I am oversimplifying here, but for example, if you can create an irrevocable trust, and you transfer your house into it, you can still live in it during your lifetime and your spouse or children will get it at your death. Wait a minute, isn't that want happens with a revocable trust? The answer is yes, it is. The difference is if you and your spouse transfer your house to an irrevocable trust now, and that trust says it is going to your children at the death of you and your spouse, you can't change that, whereas in a revocable trust you could change the beneficiaries at your death to anyone you pleased.

If you are like most people you might be saying: "But Reed, I'm not going to not change my beneficiaries. My children are going to get whatever is left of our estate and we aren't going to change that." In the case of Medi-Cal planning in California, if you transfer your home into an irrevocable trust, the state can't put a lien on the home after your death to recover what they have paid for your benefit to a nursing home.*

Then why wouldn't you just transfer your home to an irrevocable trust now since nothing is going to change in your estate plan and your children are always going to be your beneficiaries? Or, you may be asking why not just give my house to my children now, and they can let me live in it. Many people do this with dire consequences.

First, if you are married we don't know who is going into a nursing home, if anyone. So, if you transfer your home into an irrevocable trust and make your kids the trustees and beneficiaries you have limited the options you have with that home. For example, you may wish to get an equity line of credit, refinance a mortgage, or get a reverse mortgage, and these things can be much harder (if not impossible) to do once you have put the kids in control. It would be a better idea to wait until you know you or your spouse need long term care, and then transfer the home out of the incapacitated spouse's name into an irrevocable trust for the benefit of the well spouse. This leaves the well spouse in charge so he or she can do what they need to.

You never want to give your home directly to your children to avoid a creditor for two big reasons. The first reason is taxes. If you transfer your home directly to your children while you are alive they get the same cost basis in your home as you do. This is called a carryover basis under Section 1015 of the Internal Revenue Code. That means that when your children sell the home they will subtract what you paid for the home (the cost or "basis"- let's say $100,000) from the selling price (let's say $1,000,000). This means they will have a capital gain of $900,000. Depending on what state they live in their taxes in the sale of that home could be as high as $270,000.

If you instead give the home to an irrevocable trust, and that trust has the right language to meet the requirements of the Internal Revenue Code, then your children could get the home at your death, sell it, and pay ZERO taxes. They could get a step-up in basis under Section 1014 of the Internal Revenue Code which means they get a new cost basis at your death equal to the fair market value of the home at your death. In this scenario, the fair market value is the selling price of $1,000,000, so the new cost basis would be $1,000,000. The selling price is $1,000,000 so the profit is Zero (selling price=$1,000,000 – Stepped-up cost basis of $1,000,000=profit of ZERO=NO TAX).

The second big reason not to transfer your home directly to your children (or put them on as joint tenants), is so it can't be lost in a divorce or some other financial setback that may happen to your child. Once your child is on title your home is exposed to whatever happens in your child's life.

The irrevocable trust lets you keep the tax benefits in your home, it protects the home from creditors or state Medi-Cal recovery, and allows you to continue to use it. But since we don't know which spouse might need Medi-Cal benefits we may not want to set this trust up until we know who needs it. The problem with waiting is incapacity. Most traditional estate plans and powers-of-attorney do not give you the legal authority to set up an irrevocable trust for an incapacitated spouse.

As I mentioned in the previous section, California Probate Code Section 4264 says that a power of attorney must specifically grant the authority to allow the agent (a well spouse) to create an irrevocable trust and fund that trust with property of the principal (the ill spouse). **This is why the previous section on Medicaid Triggers is so critical to asset protection planning. With the right language in your existing documents you can protect your assets. Without the right language, you may have to kiss your assets goodbye.**

* As of January 1, 2017, California has issued new guidelines saying they will not try to recover against a home that is not going through probate. The means a home that transfers to a spouse or to children at death through an ordinary removable trust should be safe from recovery. The problem with depending on this is that you are at the whims of the state and the recovery rules could change back at any moment. I do not advise my clients to put their assets at the discretion of legislative or bureaucratic whims. I still advise a transfer to an irrevocable trust in most cases.

You Need a Trust Protector

Is that it? Is language allowing me to do the types of things I need to do for Medicaid planning all I need to have in my documents to make a "modern estate plan"? Unfortunately, no. The title of this chapter is "The Secret Is Flexibility," and that means that a good estate plan must also be flexible enough to keep up with changes in the law and changes with your family.

For example, what if the way you need to qualify for Medicaid changes completely, or the state requires you to have something else in your documents before you can apply? What if you are incapacitated and you aren't in a position to update your documents? Is court inevitable? Not if a very important section called a "Trust Protector" is in your documents.

64

A Trust Protector Provision is the central part of any modern estate and asset protection plan. It protects your family from almost anything that may happen in the future, whether there is a new tax law, a change in the healthcare law, a change in your family circumstances, or any number of things that are hard for us to anticipate.

As important as the Trust Protector Provision is, very few attorneys are familiar with it or include it in their estate planning documents. In fact, one attorney confided to me that he doesn't like to include it since he knows he will make less money in court fees. The Trust Protector Provision almost always means the family does not have to go to court to fix anything!

A Trust Protector Provision is a lot more than protection from devastating healthcare expenses. It also protects your family from any number of events that you didn't count on.

For example, let's say that you and your spouse leave your estate equally to your two children. What happens if one of your children has a child (your grandchild) with autism or some other special needs? Your grandchild with autism may not even be born when you created your estate plan; he or she could be born after you die. What happens then if your child, the parent of the special needs grandchild, dies and the money ends up being inherited by the special needs grandchild?

If this were to happen, your special needs grandchild would be thrown off any government healthcare or special needs assistance he or she might be receiving, until the money inherited was spent to zero.

Most trusts do not accommodate unforeseen circumstances such as this. In a circumstance such as this, the only option would be for your grandchild to be thrown off government assistance until his or her inheritance was depleted, or to go through a costly and difficult court proceeding to try and get the court to set up a special needs trust. However, if your trust had a Trust Protector Provision, your successor trustee could avoid a court proceeding and instead appoint a Trust

Protector to create a special needs trust for your grandchild without going to court.

The Trust Protector is typically an experienced estate planning attorney selected by your successor trustee. The attorney will look at the trust and see that he or she has the authority to convert the inheritance for your grandchild into a special needs trust so the grandchild can keep the inheritance without losing any valuable government benefits he or she might be receiving or otherwise be eligible for.

All of this can be done by the Trust Protector without having to go to court and explain things to a judge. Your Trustee doesn't need permission, because you already gave it to him or her when you included the authority in your documents for a Trust Protector to change the trust to protect your beneficiaries if there was a change in circumstances just like this.

The Trust Protector could be the original drafting attorney, but it doesn't have to be. It can be any attorney with experience in trust administration.

This is just one example of the power of the Trust Protector Provision. We also need this provision in your documents for you and your spouse. Even though a trust can be drafted for you with Medicaid Triggers today, the state probate code may change and the Medicaid Triggers in the future may look completely different. Without a Trust Protector Provision, your family will be in court hoping for a sympathetic judge.

If the federal tax law changes, your Trust Protector can change your documents to comply with the new law. As recently as the tax laws have been changing lately, this one example alone could save your family hundreds of thousands of dollars.

Designing flexibility into your documents, and building in trapdoors and protection provisions, can protect your family from devastating healthcare expenses. They can also protect your family from state and federal tax laws as well as asset confiscation laws that weren't even in existence when your plan was initially designed.

And, of course, don't forget the changes that can occur in your own family circumstances. A flexible design allows your successor trustee to take private action to protect your family without having to ask the state for permission. After all, isn't the purpose of an estate plan to avoid the court system, unnecessarily frustration, expenses, and taxes?

Make Sure Your Plan Works as Intended

The problem is that many people try to cut corners when they do their estate planning or they simply don't know what to ask. Remember the question that I get most often from people calling into my office: "How much for a trust?" Hopefully by now you are starting to see that this is probably not the right question. A better question might be: "If you design an estate plan for my family, will it actually accomplish what I expect it to?"

Ask about how the plan design protects your family from devastating healthcare costs, and how it ensures your family will actually receive and keep their inheritance.

In the next chapter we'll take on the next big enemy of modern estate planning, but first I want to make one last comment about designing flexibility into your estate plan. Many of my clients are surprised to see the size of the estate plan I design and prepare for them. While it is certainly true that long, thick documents are not always necessary or even well written, it is important if we are going to have the kind of flexibility and asset protection that will guarantee your family has options when needed.

No one knows exactly what is going to happen, so I put all the tools I can possibly think of into your toolbox (your estate plan) just in case you need them. If I don't put them in before you have a devastating healthcare crisis, or there's a tax law change, or a change in your family's circumstances, it will be too late. Think about it for a minute. If your car broke down by the side of the road, and you called your mechanic to come out and fix the car, you wouldn't tell him to only bring his screwdriver, would you? Of course not, you'd insist he bring all the tools he has in his truck, because you don't want to spend any more time on the side of the road than absolutely necessary.

Time to move on to the next destroyer of your estate plan. Pleases note just because I have chosen to cover this second doesn't necessarily mean it is second in importance. In fact, based on my experience, the next enemy probably destroys more estate plans and causes more weeping and gnashing of teeth than any other single thing that can happen to your family. Yet again, it is almost completely ignored in most trusts and estate plans.

Section III
"Oh, I'd Never Get Married Again"

"The first time you marry for love, the second for money, and
the third for companionship."
~ Jackie Kennedy

Chapter 5
Just the Facts

It's funny, but when I meet with a married couple to design their estate plan, they tend to think in terms of what happens to their children after they both die, but they almost never think about what happens when just one dies first and the survivor lives for another 10, 20, or even 30 years. The scenarios I am about to describe are exactly why this disconnect between planning and reality may be THE biggest enemy of modern estate planning.

This is something I address in all my planning sessions, because it is what happens after the death of the first spouse that will determine whether your children will even have an inheritance!

The assumption married couples make when they do their planning is that one of them will die, and the surviving spouse will live alone for a few years and then die, and of course what's left of the couple's lifetime of hard work and savings will be used to help make life a little easier for their children and grandchildren.

That may have been true a hundred years ago when the average life span was 50, but now with an average life span approaching 80, that is not smart planning. In a modern estate and asset protection plan, if you aren't designing a plan that will protect your children from a remarriage by your spouse, then you may just want to give your money to your children now, because that is the only way you can be sure it will go to your children and not your spouse's new stepchildren!

People need to know the fact that the types of estate planning they are doing hasn't been keeping up with what actually eats up family wealth. Most people and even most attorneys are still designing plans that are meant to protect against taxes and death probates, but those types of things just aren't a factor in today's world. Now one of the biggest enemies of your family's wealth is the fact that your spouse is likely to remarry after your death, and the longer he or she lives after your death, the higher the probability that none of your estate will make it to your children.

Married couples almost always say the same thing: "Oh, if I survive Sally (or Bob), I would never get married again." That may be the politically correct thing to say in front of your spouse in your attorney's office, but if you want to actually protect your children and grandchildren (and your spouse), then you need to plan for reality.

Statistically more than 60 percent of men and approximately 20 percent of women are involved in a new romance or remarried within just over two years of being widowed, according to the article "Dating and Remarriage over the First Two Years of Widowhood" (*Annals of Clinical Psychiatry,* 8, 51-57).

My own mother remarried within five years after my father's death, and my parents had been married for 40 years.
The younger the widow or widower is, the higher the probability that they will remarry; the longer that second marriage lasts, the higher the probability that the children of the first marriage will not get an inheritance.

So what happens to the inheritance? Are there a bunch of predators out there just waiting to prey on widows and widowers? Yes, and that is one reason I see fortunes rerouted to unintended beneficiaries. The reasons I see most often, however, for children from the first marriage not receiving a dime are that the remarried parent is either careless or foolish, and they die before their new spouse. Let me give you some real-life examples of cases I have seen to illustrate my point.

The Trusting Wife

Bill and Sue were a very happily married couple, and they had four children they both loved very much. Bill was a successful businessman and Sue had been a homemaker for their four children that they raised together over their 40-year marriage.

Sue was a loving and supportive wife, outgoing, and attractive, and her social skills helped Bill gain support for his business in the community. Their four children were all healthy adults living their own lives when Bill died of a heart attack at 65. Sue was five years younger than Bill, and even though she was devastated by his death, she was not the type to be depressed. She had many friends and social contacts, and there were many men in the community who considered her attractive and fun to be with.

As smart and engaged as Sue was, she had never handled the finances in the household. She had left that all to Bill. She had plenty of money to live on, as Bill had built a substantial business, but she really wasn't that savvy about the day-to-day finances. Within two years of Bill's death, Sue had met a new man who she was completely in love with. He was 10 years younger than Sue, but that didn't seem to matter to him, and besides, Sue really was more attractive than most women 10 or even 15 years younger than her, and it seemed all the men her own age were either in poor health or boring. Plus, her new man was great with finances and was willing to take over the mundane tasks that she didn't like doing. She had even been introduced to him by their financial advisor, so she felt like she could trust him. Within 12 months of their first date, they had a beautiful wedding in Hawaii. His two adult children and her four adult children were all there as one big happy new family.

Sue and her new husband, Phil, had a great life together. Sue was a sweet woman without a care in the world. She now had someone who liked dealing with all the financial stuff to look out for her, and she could concentrate on traveling and seeing the world with Phil. As much as Sue had loved Bill, he was always working, and never wanted to travel and see the world like she did. She hated to admit it to herself, but Phil was just a lot more interesting and fun to be with than Bill.

Sue's time to pass from this world came when she was 82. She felt fortunate: she had been blessed with two wonderful husbands and four beautiful children who had given her 10 beautiful grandchildren. She died in her sleep comforted by the fact that she left behind a loving family that would remember her fondly as their loving mom and grandmother.

What Sue hadn't realized or even thought to care about, however, was that Phil had exclusive control of their finances for over 20 years. When Phil had met Sue, he was a little down on his luck. He was recently divorced, and his first wife had cleaned him out pretty good. Even though he believed he really did love Sue, she couldn't have come along at a better time. She was a rich widow with several million dollars, and she had no desire to be burdened with managing her affairs.

Even though Bill and Sue had created an estate plan before Bill died, all it did at Bill's death was set up an A/B trust, which was designed to keep Bill's estate tax credit in the estate. It didn't prevent Sue from spending the money in Bill's trust any way she saw fit, and it didn't prevent her from giving away her half of the estate. The trust had language that she was supposed to not go into the principal of Bill's trust unless she needed it for her health, maintenance, and support, but since she was the trustee, who was going to question her right to spend her own money? Her children didn't know what she was doing; they assumed their father had set things up to protect their mom and them, and besides, they were just happy that mom was happy.

Over Sue and Phil's 20-year marriage, Phil had managed to get all of the assets in Sue's estate put into joint tenancy accounts (including the valuable family ranch). He told Sue this was easier, because that way either one of them could be in control. Sue didn't want Phil to be out in the cold if something happened to her, and she trusted Phil with all the financial things, so she had no problem signing the things he asked her to sign (remember they had been married several years before any of this happened, so Sue had really grown to think of Phil as her protector).

Even though Sue and Bill's estate was worth well over $4 million dollars at the time of Bill's death, Sue and Bill's children were surprised to find out that they were only going to inherit the $500,000 that was left in Bill's trust. When Bill had died, $2 million dollars had been put in Bill's trust (his half of the estate at the time of his death). But Sue did like to travel and Phil had always told her it was better to use the money in Bill's trust first because that's what it was there for: to pay for her expenses.

Sue's children were surprised to find out that Sue's half of the estate, which included the family ranch (worth over a million dollars) and another $1 million of stocks, had been taken out of her trust and put in joint tenancy with Phil. When Sue died Phil became the sole owner of those assets, and her trust was no longer controlling. Phil was the owner of the joint tenancy assets by operation of law.

The children were pretty upset with Phil and decided to see a lawyer to see if they could get Sue's half of the estate back. The lawyer had to tell them that it did not look good for them. They could try and argue that Phil used undue influence to take advantage of Sue, but that would be hard to show since Sue had never shown any signs of dementia, Alzheimer's, or another condition to support that theory. The lawyer explained that while Sue did violate the trust terms by using the money in Bill's trust and not her own trust, it would be hard for them to get the money back since it wasn't in Sue's trust anymore to make an argument for redistribution. The assets and been put in joint tenancy, and they were now owned by Phil. Sue had been the trustee of Bill's trust, and she had signed on the checks on the accounts in that trust. Phil had never personally taken any money out of Bill's trust, so the children would have to show that Phil tricked or unduly influenced Sue to take the money out—again, a very hard thing to prove with these facts. Sue had a right to do whatever she wanted with the assets in her survivor's trust, and the fact that she took them out of the trust and put them in joint tenancy with her husband was not by itself evidence of fraud or undue influence. The lawyer told Bill and Sue's children that based on the facts he was not willing to take this case on contingency, but if they wanted to pay him a sizeable retainer and then be prepared to replenish it as he used it up with his billable hours that he'd be happy to see what he could do. "Who knows," he said: "Maybe Phil would be willing to pay you a couple of hundred thousand just to get you to go away."

Needless to say, when Bill and Sue went to their very respected estate planning lawyer to design their estate plan, they weren't expecting this outcome, and yet this is one of the biggest, if not *the* biggest, enemies of many people's estate plans today.

Do you think if Bill could look down from above and see that Sue (with the help of Phil) had casually transferred his 40 years of sweat and hard work to a perfect stranger, that he might have been kicking himself for spending so much time at the office? Would he like to do his estate plan over? I'll bet he would, and I'm going to show you how in the next chapter.

Before I show you how to make sure this doesn't happen to you, however, I want to make just a couple of important points.

In case you think this is an unlikely scenario, the above story is a composite of a number of real cases. It is not at all unlikely or even uncommon.

Also, I intentionally used an example where the wife is the survivor, because often people are more familiar with a surviving husband remarrying and cutting out the children of the first marriage in favor of his new spouse. I wanted to use this example to illustrate that it can happen to both sexes, and both spouses need to be concerned about it in their planning.

The statistic at the beginning of this chapter that showed that 60 percent of men remarry within two years of becoming a widow doesn't mean that women can't also be guilty of losing the family inheritance.

I could fill this book with examples of men who have remarried and for any number of reasons cut out the children from the first marriage (like the high-profile Anna Nicole Smith case). In fact, I recently had a widowed client bring his new wife into my office. I sat there in awe at how good she was at subtlety manipulating him to rewrite his plan to include her children from her first marriage. I had helped him and his first wife design their estate plan before she died. Unfortunately, his first wife didn't think she needed to include the provision I am about to discuss that could have addressed this problem. In fact, I'll never forget what they both said in unison: "We don't need that. Neither one of us would ever remarry."

> "An ounce of prevention is better than a pound of cure."
> ~ Benjamin Franklin

Chapter 6
Have Fun, but Don't Forget the Kids

While it is certainly true that you don't have to leave any inheritance to your children and grandchildren, you probably don't want everything that you worked so hard for all your life to go to complete strangers. Yes, I know, I hear it all the time: "We're going to spend everything so there won't be anything left for the kids." I hear it all the time, but I never see it.

The Surviving Spouse Protection Plan™

What I do see are a lot of estates that are set up with no protection for the surviving spouse or the children from the first marriage. As a result of this ever-increasing phenomenon, I am now recommending that married couples insert key provisions in their revocable trust that provides protection for the surviving spouse and the children from the first marriage.

I call this provision the Surviving Spouse Protection Plan™ because it protects the surviving spouse from predators and from themselves not paying attention to how the trust is managed. It also prevents a spouse from giving away the entire estate to someone else when he or she becomes older and more susceptible to the influence of new people in his or her life.

Want to take a guess as to how many times I have heard the following phrase uttered by a remarried man when he is cutting out the kids from the first marriage and including his new wife's children in his estate plan: "My kids hardly visit me anymore anyway. I have a closer relationship with my step-children."

How do we protect the surviving spouse (and your children) from this happening?

Remember throughout this book how I referred to the A/B trust? If you have a trust you may even have a trust like this; it just doesn't have the protections I am about to discuss. A/B trusts were originally designed for estate tax planning purposes. They have become less popular today, as more attorneys are using disclaimer trusts, which I'll explain more shortly.

The A/B trust is language in a trust you have with your spouse that says at the death of the first spouse the surviving spouse is *required* (not optional) to split the single trust into two trusts. One trust, the "A" trust (often called the survivor's trust) will hold assets representing the survivor's share of the estate, and the second trust, or "B" trust (often called the exemption or credit shelter Trust), will hold assets representing the deceased spouse's share of the estate.

This type of trust was the most prevalent type of trust used for married couples back when the estate tax exemption amount per person was $600,000. However, now the estate tax exemption per person is $5,250,000. This means that, unless your net worth is over $5,250,000 at your death, then your estate is not subject to estate tax. When the first spouse died and their B trust was set up by the surviving spouse, the B trust became irrevocable, meaning the surviving spouse could not change the terms or the beneficiaries of the B trust. The A trust is still revocable and amendable because it belongs to the survivor, and since he or she is still alive, the surviving spouse can do whatever he or she wants with that share but is not allowed to change beneficiaries of the deceased spouse's share (the B trust).

Of course, most people will have the surviving spouse as the sole trustee of both the A and the B trusts, so you are still trusting the surviving spouse to not spend all of the B trust's assets or give them away to a new spouse.

Since the estate tax exemption amount has risen to over $5,000,000 per person, and since you can now keep a deceased spouse's estate tax exemption without a credit shelter trust at all, many attorneys are drafting what are called "disclaimer trusts," which essentially states that everything goes to the surviving spouse and the surviving spouse can change beneficiaries, or give it all to a new spouse, or whatever else they want with no restrictions to remember the children from the first marriage.

Why would an attorney recommend a disclaimer trust and eliminate what little protection was available to protect the surviving spouse from predators and to protect the children from the first marriage?

The answer is what I said at the beginning of the book: Many attorneys and financial advisors are only approaching your planning from the traditional death and taxes perspective. They are not creating modern estate plans designed to protect your family from the real enemies of your hard-earned savings.

The more important question is: How can we protect your family? I gave you this brief explanation of trusts so I can now tell you how I solve the problem of your surviving spouse intentionally or unintentionally disinheriting your children.

The Surviving Spouse Protection Plan™ is designed to protect your surviving spouse and your children, and it works by taking the old A/B trust concept and bringing it up-to-date.

Under the Surviving Spouse Protection Plan™ at the death of the first spouse the surviving spouse is required to set up the B trust, and it will hold the deceased spouses share of the estate. That means that the children of the first marriage are the irrevocable beneficiaries of that trust. However, you could see from the example of Bill, Sue, and Sue's new husband, Phil, that having an A/B trust by itself does not prevent the surviving spouse from using all those assets for her new spouse. So how do we fix that?

We add a provision that says the surviving spouse can act as sole trustee of the B trust for the rest of his or her life. The surviving spouse can have access to the income and principal if needed, but we also say that if he or she should ever remarry, he or she is required to get a premarital agreement with their fiancé/fiancée. What happens if he or she doesn't? We can give the surviving spouse some choices. We could say that if he or she gets married without a premarital agreement, then he or she can no longer be the sole trustee of the B trust and that one of the adult children (or someone else you trust or a bank trustee) will now serve as co-trustee with the surviving spouse as co-trustee of the B trust. This prevents the surviving spouse from being influenced to use up the money in the B trust.

Or, we could have an even harsher penalty for not getting a premarital agreement: We could say that if he or she gets married without a pre-marital agreement then the entire B trust will go to the children.

Please note that we are not saying that the surviving spouse can't get married. A provision saying your spouse couldn't get married would be unenforceable, as it is against a public policy that promotes marriage. You can, however, say that a premarital agreement is required. This is not against public policy, as you are not preventing a marriage; you are simply saying what happens to your money if there is not a premarital agreement that will protect your children from the first marriage.

You may be asking yourself a practical question at this point: How do the children know this provision requiring a premarital agreement on the part of their mother or father is required? What is to prevent a surviving spouse from simply getting remarried without a pre-marital agreement?

The answer is simple: tell your children this provision is part of your plan. That is the best way. Otherwise they may not know that they have a right to require this. Remember, it's not just them they are protecting; this provision protects the surviving spouse as well. It protects them from predators that may be out to take advantage of them as well as just becoming more susceptible to influence as they become older.

It is awful to have to face the horrible truth, but it's a fact. I have seen it much too often in my practice. Clients who were brilliant in their prime lose their ability to make good choices as they get into 80s and 90s, and yet these are the years when people make the most changes in their estate plans.

The Surviving Spouse Protection Plan™ is how to make sure your family doesn't suffer from the "Cinderella Effect," a lifetime of savings going to someone other than your children.

Protect Your Children

So that's it, right? We've now dealt with making sure that everything we worked so hard to accumulate during our lifetimes gets to the people we love and care about. We've talked about how remarriages can destroy the best intentions of a married couple, and I showed you a practical and workable solution that can save your children's (and maybe grandchildren's) inheritance. What else is there? After all, if your children are adults you can't do anything more for them, right? Besides, if they don't know how to take of themselves by now, then there's nothing you can do. Isn't that what people say?

Your children being adults doesn't make them immune to things that can happen through no fault of their own—things like divorce, financial setbacks, bankruptcy, or dying before their spouse so that their spouse can remarry and give away your estate.

You may have heard the expression "You can't control things from the grave." Well, I don't know if that is true, but I do know you can *protect* your children and your grandchildren from beyond the grave, and it's very simple to do—so simple, in fact, I am still puzzled every day why everyone doesn't include the provisions I am about to show you in their estate plans.

Section IV
They're on Their Own Now

"For in the final analysis, our most basic common link, is that we all inhabit this small planet, we all breathe the same air, we all cherish our children's futures, and we are all mortal."

~ John F. Kennedy

Chapter 7
Smart People Get Divorced, Too

If I told you there was a simple way to protect your children from divorces, creditors, bankruptcies, lawsuits, and other things that might come their way, you'd probably want to know about it, wouldn't you? After all, we already know you care about your family - that's why you're reading this book. But what if I told you that your children couldn't get this protection for themselves—only you can give it to them as a once-in-a-lifetime gift?

The Dynasty Protection Trust ™

What if I then told you that the cost and the effort involved in giving this incredible gift to you children was so miniscule that you wouldn't even notice the difference? Well, that is exactly what I am telling you, and the incredible, once-in-a-lifetime gift that only you can give is called an inheritance trust.

Most people, when designing their estate plans, only worry about taking care of their kids until they reach a certain age. For example, if your children are under 18, you might say in your trust, "My trustee can hold my child's share in trust for my child's benefit until they are 25 and then my trustee shall give my child their inheritance outright and free of trust." Maybe your attorney got really clever and your trust says, "My child can get a third of their inheritance at 25, half the remainder at 30, and the final distribution at 35." The problem with this language is that once the distribution is made the assets are exposed to whatever evils may befall your child, such as predators, creditors, and lawsuits.

Is it possible that a 36-year-old child could get divorced? Or could a child get divorced and remarried, and end up with some step-children you didn't even meet before you died?

The divorce rate for first marriages is 50 percent, and in case you believe that love is lovelier the second time around bear in mind that the divorce rate for remarriages is 60 percent (from the article, "Remarried with Children" by Mila Koumpilava, from The Forum from Fargo, North Dakota, September 12, 2006).

Separate or Community Property?

The problem is if you give your children their inheritance "out-right and free of trust at any age," then their inheritance could be gone quicker than their spouse's attorney says "community property." Many people know that what you inherit is considered your separate property. What most people fail to realize, however, is that the longer your children are married after they receive an inheritance, the harder it is for them to argue separate property in a divorce. Let me give you an example to illustrate what I mean.

At the death of you and your spouse, you leave your 40-year-old son $500,000 outright and free of trust. He puts it in a separate bank account with only his name on the account. Pretty easy—sepa-rate property, right? Over the next five years, he uses that account to buy things for the house he owns with his wife (new roof, remodeled kitchens and bathrooms, etc.). He uses the account to pay for family vacations and other things that he and his wife enjoy. Your son's wife has a job and also contributes to the household expenses.

Five years later your son's wife files for divorce, and her law-yer wants half of that account that is in your son's name. Does she have a case? It depends. First of all, her lawyer will argue that he was only able to keep the account separate because the wife contributed to the household expenses and paid for many things with her money. Secondly, he will argue that by your son's actions he intended that the account be community property because he used it almost exclusively as a community account. He used it to remodel the community house and used it for family vacations, and in fact he didn't really use it for anything other than community purposes. Further, the wife will probably say that her husband told her on more than one occasion that he considered the inheritance theirs and not just his.

That is how an inheritance gets converted into community property without even trying. It's gone before you know it, and all of that could have been prevented with a little thoughtful planning.

Most trusts have language in them that distributions shall be made "outright and free of trust," and this language is, in my opinion, the most dangerous language you can have in a trust document today.

I know what you are saying at this point: "But I don't want to hold my children's assets in trust for them for their entire life. Who would be the trustee, a bank or a relative? I don't want my 35- or 45-year-old child to have ask a bank or a relative for money when they need it. My child is mature enough to manage his own money." Those are all good points, and that is exactly why your children are going to be in charge of their own money and inheritance, but the way I'm going to show you allows them the best of both worlds: They are going to be in total control with total protection.

We give your children the precious gift of a protected inheritance over which they have total control through a vehicle known as a beneficiary controlled inheritance trust. This is the crown jewel in the modern estate and asset protection plan, and if you don't leave your children their inheritance in this way, it will be exposed to any number of things that destroy inheritances, not just divorce. (The average inheritance in the United States is gone within 18 months of receipt by a beneficiary.)

The way to get this protection for your children is to create their inheritance trust within your own trust. This works by adding language to your trust that says when your children get their inheritance, instead of it being distributed to them "outright and free of trust," children will instead have their shares distributed to them in their own Dynasty Protection Trust™ or personal inheritance trust. If your children are old enough to be in control of their own inheritance, then they can be trustees of their own trust, just like you were trustee of your own trust while you were alive. For example, if you were going to let your children have their inheritance outright and free of trust at 25, then you would simply say: "My child will be trustee of his own trust if he has attained the age of 25."

A child who is serving as trustee of his or her own trust is in complete control, meaning he or she can take as much money or assets out of the trust whenever he or she likes, but at the same time the language of the trust protects him or her from divorce, creditors, and lawsuits.

Your child is in complete control and doesn't need anyone's permission to take assets out of the trust. However, if your child should get in really serious trouble (for example, hits and kills a bicyclist with his or her car), your child can prevent a court from compelling him or her to turn over the assets of the trust by bringing in a corporate co-trustee that can "lock down" the trust assets so they can only be used for your child's benefit and not paid out to anyone else. This special provision acts like an invisible guardian ready to act if needed, but not even noticeable if your child never needs it.

I build in additional asset protection language into your children's trusts—language that gives them the maximum protection under the law. Upon your death, their trusts became irrevocable (i.e., can't be changed), which is what makes the trust so powerful in protecting their inheritance, and it the reason that only you can give them this gift.

An irrevocable trust can provide excellent asset protection if it was not created by the beneficiary (your child). For example, if you give your children their inheritance outright and then they try to protect themselves from divorce by transferring the inheritance into an irrevocable trust that they created, the courts will go through that trust like the big bad wolf through a straw house. However, the courts respect and honor the language of an irrevocable trust of parents who leave their children their inheritance in such a manner.

Why do the courts respect these types of trusts more than others? Because the trust was created as a part of your estate plan, it was your money not your child's, and the trust says that your child is just the lifetime beneficiary and at his or her death it was your desire to have the trust assets go to your grandchildren by that child. This is a key element to remember. You have said as a part of your estate plan that you are creating a multi-generational trust that you intend to eventually get to your grandchildren. It doesn't matter if you even have grandchildren yet; the mere fact that you have told the court that this is a multi-generational trust is alerting them to the fact that the trust should not be interfered because of whatever is going on in the life of your child. The courts have a long history of respecting and not inter fering with people's estate plans, and if they took money away from your child it would have no chance to get to your grandchildren, would it?

There are many reasons why the Dynasty Protection Trust™ works so well: the special asset protection language, the irrevocability at your death, and the fact that it has a multi-generational purpose. All these things combined make the inheritance trust the best asset protection money can buy, and will give your children a peace of mind that they cannot buy for themselves. If you don't include this gift in your estate plan, it can never be regained by your children or grandchildren after your death. If you don't use it now, it is gone forever.

You may be saying to yourself, "You know this guy doesn't know my family. I don't care what the statistics say. He doesn't know what a sweet person my daughter-in-law (or son-in-law) is. My daughter-in-law is so sweet that she would never divorce my son. Plus, all this talk about creditors and lawsuits is nonsense. My family doesn't get involved in things like that."

Well, then, you are certainly a lucky family, and I congratulate you on your good fortune. Regardless of whether you believe your children will ever get divorced, or have a lawsuit or creditor problem, however, you may still want to have a Dynasty Protection Trust™ for the reason I am going to discuss in the next chapter.

> **"Left to themselves, if something can go wrong it will."**
> **~ The First Corollary of Murphy's Law**

Chapter 8
I Hope You Like Your
Step-Grandkids

When you were fighting traffic to get to work and then once at to work putting up with things you'd rather not put up with, I'll bet you never suspected that all that effort was so that when you died you could leave your life's savings to perfect strangers. I think most people would like to think that whatever money they hadn't used on themselves during their lifetime would be used to lighten the burden on their family after they've gone. Based on my experience, I think most people would be very disappointed to see what actually happens to their lifetime of hard work and effort.

In the previous chapter, I showed you what can happen if you leave your children their inheritance "outright and free of trust." Or at least I showed you some of what can happen: Divorces, creditors, and lawsuits can take away what you hoped would be something that could make your family's life a little easier.

Perfect Strangers

But I left something out of the previous chapter—something that is going to happen to your children regardless of whether they ever get divorced, sued, or have a creditor problem. That's right. Even if you believe your children are never going to get divorced, sued, or have a creditor problem, there is one thing I am certain is going to happen to your children. I am certain because it happens to all of us. Eventually, we all die.

You knew that, though. Everyone dies; that's not new information. But did you know when you leave your money to your children "outright and free of trust," you have just increased the probability that the inheritance you leave your children will go to someone other than your family?

Let's imagine that after both you and your spouse die you would like what is left of your estate to go to your son. Your son has two children (your grandchildren). You love your grandchildren very much, and you thought about making them a specific gift in your estate plan, but you decided instead to just leave everything to your son, because you knew he would use some of the inheritance to take care of your grandchildren.

You have a wonderful daughter-in-law. She is a sweetheart and everyone loves her. Your son and your daughter-in-law have a perfect marriage and you are sure that they will never divorce. You were so confident of this, in fact, that you ignored my advice about leaving your son's inheritance to him in an inheritance trust. You decided to just leave him everything outright and free of trust.

After you and your spouse leave this world, your son receives his inheritance, and he and his family are very grateful. Your son wisely invests the money and saves it so that he can retire early and spend more time with his children. Unfortunately, your son doesn't quite make it to retirement. He died of a heart attack at just 50 years old.

Your son was such a hard worker, in fact, that he never took time off to take care of his own personal affairs, like getting an estate plan. Even though you had reminded him several times, he never could find the time. However, at least he put a beneficiary designation on the investment account where he kept his inheritance. Guess who his beneficiary was? That's right: your sweet daughter-in-law. Whew—what a relief! Now there won't be a probate, and you trust your daughter-in-law as much as your son, so there's no problem, right?

Wrong! Your daughter-in-law is a sweet woman. She's attractive, too. In fact, she's so sweet and attractive that she there are plenty of guys who are interested in her. Your daughter-in-law is lonely after your son dies, plus she never liked to take care of the finances or pay bills; that was your son's area. Now that your son isn't around she needs someone to do the stuff she doesn't like dealing with—you know, that money stuff. It isn't long before your daughter-in-law gets married again (remember - you're not here to help, you died before your son did.). Her new husband is a great guy, and he has two children of his own. In fact, they're about the same age as your grandkids (13 and 16). Just getting ready for college.

Your daughter-in-law and her new husband are a perfect match. She takes care of the kids, and he takes care of the finances. In fact, he decides it would be a good idea to just put all their accounts in their joint names so that if anything ever happened to one of them the survivor would have immediate access to the funds to take care of the family. Your daughter-in-law grew up watching *The Brady Bunch* and she thought this was wonderful. Everybody was just one big happy family.

You know what comes next, don't you? Well, any number of things could happen. For instance, your daughter-in-law and her new hubby could get a divorce, in which case half of what should have gone to your grandchildren is now going to your "step-grandchildren." I know they aren't really your step-grandchildren. I'm just trying to make a point. The point is half of your life's savings is going to complete strangers. A lot of hours on the freeway and at the office so you could pay for some stranger's kids' college. Not what you had in mind, is it?

Beware of Joint Tenancy

A divorce is one scenario, but your grandchildren aren't so lucky. Your daughter-in-law doesn't get divorced; she gets cancer.

She dies and upon her death all her joint accounts go immediately to her new hubby—including the inheritance that you had left your son "outright and free of trust." Now this total and complete stranger is going to decide whether he is going to use your money for your grandchildren's education or if he is going to treat them like Cinderella. Maybe they can go to community college. After all, your daughter-in-law's new hubby has to live, too, right? He can't be wasting all of "his" money on four kids going to college all at the same time.

What would have happened in this scenario if my clients had incorporated a Dynasty Protection Trust™ into their estate plan? What would have happened is that their wishes would have been carried out, because the inheritance trust says that if their son dies his inheritance is held in trust for the benefit of his children, *not* his spouse. You may love your daughter-in-law, but that doesn't mean you want your grandchildren's inheritance to be put at risk.

You could even say that your daughter-in-law could be the trustee of your grandchildren's inheritance. The difference is she won't be able to give it away, and her new hubby won't be able to retitle it into a joint account. If you're not sure your daughter-in-law is able to manage money, then you can have another trusted family member or a bank act as trustee for your grandchildren until they are old enough. The one thing you definitely don't want to do, however, is leave your family's inheritance unprotected.

I hope that these last two chapters have demonstrated why I can't stand to see a trust that has the language "outright and free of trust." Remember: It's not about controlling your children; it's about protecting them. The old default language of trusts saying that children will get their inheritance outright is one of the most careless things you can do in your estate plan—especially when it is so simple to leave your children the ultimate protection of their own personal Dynasty Protection Trust™. The Dynasty Protection Trust™ is the best of both worlds: your child had complete control with the peace of mind of the best asset protection you can give them.

Section IV
Action

> "Act well at the moment, and you have performed
> a good action for all eternity."
> ~ Johann Kaspar Lavater

Chapter 9
How to Protect Your Family

Now that we've discussed what I believe are the three biggest enemies of your family's legacy, what can you do about it? You can now and get a modern estate and asset protection plan in place for you and your family. I've given you the questions to ask and the solutions to ask for. You are now an armed consumer who will no longer take what the attorney puts in front of you. Demand protection for your family that will actually work when needed. Don't settle for a cheap, boilerplate estate plan that looks good on the outside but doesn't protect your family from the modern threats that are devastating family wealth.

Before beginning the process of revising your current plan or designing a new plan, there are still a couple of critical things you should know. Let's review what we've talked about so far and then I will reveal the last critical factors to making sure your plan will protect your family.

We've discussed the three biggest enemies to modern estate planning and a solution to each problem:

Enemy	Solution
1. Devastating healthcare	1. Medicaid Triggers and trust protector
2. Remarriages by surviving spouse	2. Surviving Spouse Protection System™
3. Death and divorce of your children	3. Dynasty Protection Trust™

Procrastination

Even though this book has focused on the three things I believe are destroying estate plans, there are two more potential threats to your family. These two additional enemies of your planning are equally as important as the big three we've just talked about because either one of them on their own can destroy your intentions from ever being carried out. But even though they are just as important, they are a lot easier to explain so we can take care of one of them in just the next few paragraphs (and the last one in the next chapter). But don't think that just because they are easy to understand that they aren't just as devastating, because I see these two problems every day in my practice. They are procrastination and failing to keep your plan up-to-date.

I meet people every day who, when they find out what I do, say something like "Oh yeah, I need to do that" or "Yeah, I did that 10 years ago, guess I should make sure it's all in order, huh?"

The challenge with estate planning is that everyone thinks they can wait until the last minute to do it. Unfortunately, we don't know when the last minute is, do we? Also, as hopefully you've realized by now, estate planning is not just about death and taxes. Modern estate and asset protection planning needs to deal with illnesses and incapacity. These things can happen to you at any time in your life, not just when you are older. And, of course, if you have minor children and you don't have an estate plan in place appointing permanent and temporary guardians and trustees to manage their finances, then you are just, quite frankly, being foolish. So if you haven't done your planning yet, take action today. Set a goal to have it done by a specific date, and take the first step to making sure it is done. Set up an appointment with an experienced estate planning attorney who will take the time to understand your family and help you build a modern estate plan.

Once you have your estate plan in place, however, realize that times have radically changed. No longer are the days when you could visit the attorney, sign your documents, and then stick them in a safe and let your children deal with things 30 years later. That just doesn't work in our modern society. The laws are changing every year. We have new health insurance delivery systems, radically changing tax laws on both the state and federal levels. You change jobs, get new retirement accounts, and open new investment accounts, and very often those new assets are not coordinated with your estate plan. If you put your estate plan away and don't look at it for even three years, I would venture to say that it is no longer going to be up-to-date for any number of reasons. I have found that most consumers are not aware of this problem, and most attorneys have not yet developed a solution for this problem.

  So how can you easily and confidently keep your plan up-to-date? Well I have developed a solution that makes it easy and routine for my clients, and my clients love the peace of mind of knowing their family's plan is always current and ready to protect their loved ones. After all, if you've taken the time to do good planning, shouldn't you take the time to make sure it works? Having an estate plan without a maintenance plan is like buying a car and never changing the oil. In the next and last chapter, I will show you how I ensure my clients have total peace of mind.

"Surely there comes a time when counting the cost and paying the price aren't things to think about any more.
All that matters is value."

~ **James Hilton**

Chapter 10
The Biggest Change - It's an Annual Thing: The Family Protection System™

When you are looking for attorneys to help with your family's planning ask them if they have a maintenance plan to make sure your plan stays up-to-date.

A Proactive System

Be careful, because all attorneys will tell you they give you free consultations every few years to review your plan, but that is not what I mean by a real proactive maintenance plan.

A good maintenance plan will be proactive. In other words, the attorney's office will contact you every year and have a system in place for reviewing and updating your plan. A good maintenance plan means the attorney's office doesn't depend on the client to contact the attorney, but rather the attorney's staff is automatically reaching out to their clients and telling the clients exactly what they need to do to keep their plan current.

In addition, a good maintenance plan will have a set annual cost that is reasonable but takes into account that the attorney's staff and the attorney will have to perform certain tasks to keep your plan in compliance. In addition, this modest annual fee should include allowing you to make minor changes to your plan without incurring any additional attorney's costs for preparing those changes.

For example, you may wish to change trustees, or guardians, or the ages at which money is distributed to your children. You may wish to make a specific gift to a charity or a friend. Or, many people often update their healthcare wishes and agents based on new information. All of these changes will be done at no additional charge if your attorney has a reliable and systematic maintenance system in place that can accommodate these changes.

By the way, you may have noticed that a real proactive maintenance system is somewhat labor intensive. In other words, make sure the attorney you're dealing with has the staff to make sure your plan will always be kept up-to-date. Also make sure the attorney is really in the business of estate planning and trust administration. In my opinion, you don't want an attorney who is doing this on the side or as an ancillary part of his or her business. Keeping estate documents up-to-date is time consuming, and needs systems and staff in place to accommodate changes.

You can now begin to see why an attorney who does not specialize in estate planning is not going to have systems in place to provide adequate protection for your family. If the attorney is a general practitioner or practices in some other area (or operates out of his or her house and does estate plans for friends and family), then not only is it unlikely that the attorney is going to be aware of any of the issues we have discussed in this book, but he or she certainly is not going to be set up to provide the ongoing maintenance for your plan and the kind of protection for your family that can ensure a plan that works when needed.

If an attorney is charging you to keep your plan up-to-date, then he or she should also be willing to give you a written guarantee that he or she will bear the cost of fixing it if something goes wrong. You and your family shouldn't have to pay for court costs and probate fees if your plan doesn't accomplish your family's objectives.

As mentioned earlier, many attorneys are happy to sell inexpensive trusts with very little counseling or thought into whether they will work for you or not. Then they do little or nothing to make sure your assets are titled correctly or your plan is kept up-to-date. This is known as a *loss leader*. In other words, the attorney is happy to build a client base by offering cheap up-front trusts so that they can get the probate and administration fees later.

The attorney is building a huge base of recurring revenue for him- or herself by giving away the trust up-front. There is no guarantee it will accomplish your objectives, so when you or your family comes back to this attorney when something goes wrong, he or she can tell you that they have to go to court for tens of thousands of dollars. The attorney will tell you it is because you didn't title your assets correctly or keep the plan up-to-date! Ask the attorney for a written guarantee that he or she will absorb the court costs if the plan is out-of-date and your family ends up in court. I offer this guarantee to my clients and you deserve the same level of planning.

Now do you see why the question "How much for a trust?" is perhaps the worst question a client can ask when choosing an attorney to design a plan to protect your family?

"If I see an ending, I can work backward"
~ Arthur Miller

Conclusion

Thank you for taking the time to read this book. It says volumes about what kind of person you are: one who cares enough about their family to take the extra time to learn how to offer them the best possible protection. You don't just rely on hearsay and what your friends and family tell you. You've taken the time to educate yourself and gone beyond the sound bites.

I hope you found this book useful and practical, because that was my intent. The bookstores are full of books on estate planning that go into technical jargon on trusts, taxes, and estate planning in general, but I haven't been able to find anything that tells consumers what's really causing problems with their planning. I've tried to cut out the technical mumbo jumbo and talk in terms that most people care about. I hope it came across that way and not condescending.

I'd love to hear your thoughts and I'm always open to positive and helpful feedback. If you'd like to drop me a line with your comments please feel free to send them to reed@yesllp.com.

If you're a California resident and you're interested in contacting me about designing your family's estate plan, or you need help with a trust administration or probate, please feel free to contact me at the same e-mail: reed@yesllp.com. I'd be happy to walk you through the process of getting started.

If you live outside of California, I work with a network of excellent estate planning attorneys across the United States, and I can refer you to a like-minded attorney in your area.
Wishing you and your family the best,

Reed Scott

FREE THIRTY MINUTE CONSULTATION!

Now that you've read the book, if what I've said makes sense to you and you'd like to set up a modern asset protection plan for your family, and you're a California resident, then email me at reed@yesllp.com and to schedule a complimentary Skype consultation.

If you live anywhere in California we can consult, design, and deliver your asset protection plan without you having to leave your home or office. Once the plan is complete and ready to sign we can use our network of mobile notaries to come to your home or office for execution. Don't worry if you don't have all your information together. We have a system for doing this that streamlines the entire process. Showing up is 95% of success!

53984977R00070

Made in the USA
San Bernardino, CA
04 October 2017